FISH FOOD - THE BOOK OF LIFE

Fish Food - The Book of Life

Published 2017

By WoMenHead101

ISBN #978-1-387-24810-0

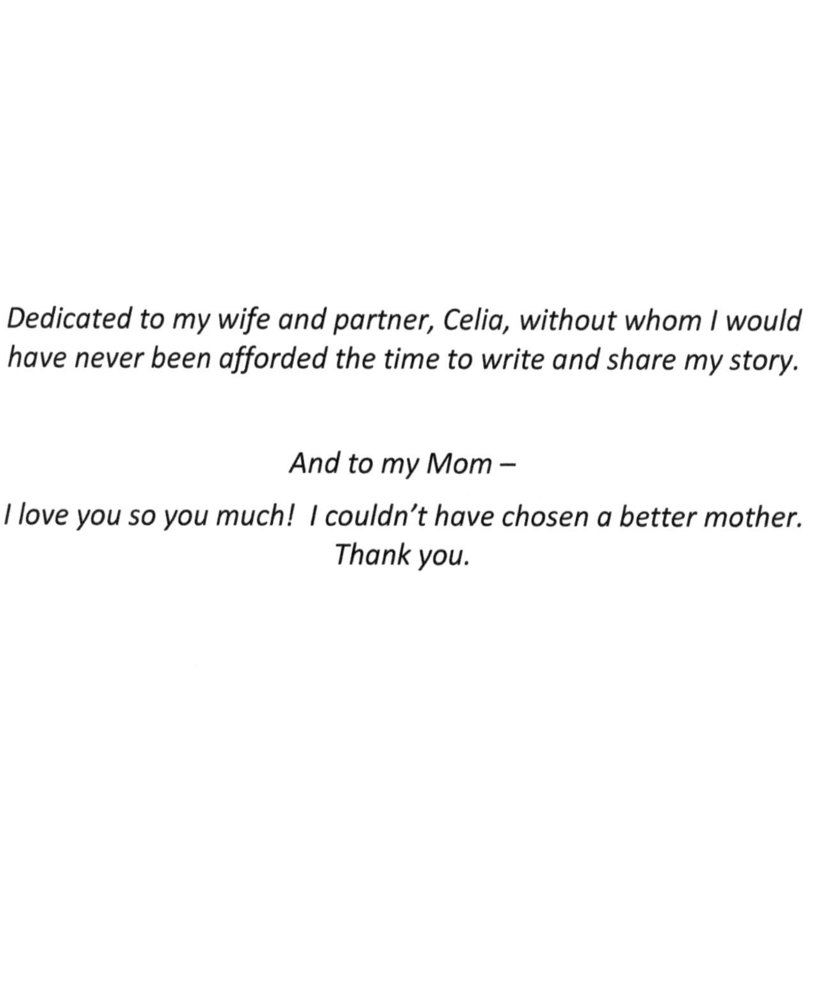

Dedicated to my wife and partner, Celia, without whom I would have never been afforded the time to write and share my story.

And to my Mom –

I love you so you much! I couldn't have chosen a better mother. Thank you.

TABLE OF CONTENTS

INTRODUCTION

This book contains many beliefs, from a variety of cultures and religions. Even though I was raised Catholic, life has taught me there is truth in all traditional spiritual beliefs.

Take Rumi for instance, he was a Persian, Sunni Muslim poet and Islamic scholar (1207 – 1273). Currently his quotes are rapidly growing in popularity here in the States. Which is a good thing, considering a number of people here in the U.S. have a negative view of Muslim's in general.

Traditional religions such as Jewish, Catholic, Hindu, Buddhist, and Muslim are all based on love; not war and murder.

> *"Buddha was not a Buddhist. Jesus was not a Christian. Muhammad was not a Muslim. They were teachers who taught love. Love was their religion."* - Unknown

So be forewarned, this is a collective book of love.

I was compelled to write this book after three surgeries (not counting the minors ones), and sixteen months with a colostomy bag hanging from my side; a total of thirty-six days in the hospital. You can say I am lucky, because I know I wanted to die at one point. It would have been much easier to do.

Two months after my final surgery to reverse the colostomy, I began a community newsletter and I passed it out in hospital waiting rooms. It was a feel good publication intended to give hope to those who felt hopeless. But I discovered that as I wrote monthly and put the articles together that I was healing myself as well as my community.

Four months later, I had a dream that I named Fish Food. The dream prompted the thought of expanding from a newsletter to a book, with the hope that a book will spread the love beyond my own community.

So I wrote about what I know - a healing journey. It's what I like to refer to as a "Holistic Fix." As I have discovered, when you're physically ill, there's more to fix than the human body. Healing involves the mind and spirit as well.

So I begin my story with the basics, what it is to be human. After all, there's nothing more dehumanizing than wearing a poop bag on your side.

At one point, I had tubes sewed into the sides of my abdomen, with these little plastic balls they called grenades that the poison drained into. One of them hung as low as my knees. First I had four, and then I had three. I had to live with these things for six weeks, along with the colostomy bag.

I would picture myself as a wicked Captain Fantastic cover with tubes floating in the air from my sides, as I championed myself standing tall on broken white ceramic tubs, toilets and sinks, with glimpses of silver water pipes here and there. It was either that or feel victimized and sorry for myself.

It most certainly was an experience that shook me to the core, quite literally. And I wouldn't change a minute of it. Otherwise I would not be the person I am today. The magic inside has been rekindled, and the fire glows.

It is my hope that the peace and magic I have found shines through to you in the form of written words wrapped in white – I present to you, "Fish Food."

CHAPTER ONE - SHRIMP OR FISH?

I dreamed I was in bed eating shrimp. There were other people there too. But later I was by myself sleeping. When I woke up it was late, it was one o'clock in the afternoon. I wanted to shower, but didn't.

Something happens and the cops are looking for me. We leave the hotel. Someone else is driving; a lady. We're in a jeep. I go to eat some shrimp when I notice it's actually one raw silver fish (head and all) in my hand. Large compared to a shrimp; six by three inches easy. I'm shocked but I eat it any way. I eat it in one bite, like a seal. I feel good!

We're looking for a new hotel.

Sometimes it can be really hard to live up to our full potential. I've been talking to God since I was child. I used to call my God side, my shadow side, because the shadow side is generally the side we hide away from others. But in the past ten years or so I have been slowly crawling out of my cave, becoming more of who I really am. I'm a big fish now, and this dream is my calling.

> *"One meets his destiny often in the road he takes to avoid it." – French Proverb*

I have learned to trust myself by erasing the clouds of doubt, like the shrimp that resemble little pieces of the mind. And defensive walls that had once shrouded me from me from my fears continue to crumble from around my heart.

The older I get, the more I love this Earth life. Youth may have its beauty, but with age comes the wisdom that unlocks the magic. Like the plants and trees, we cultivate and grow.

> *"Wisdom begins with wonder." - Socrates*

It is with the eyes of a child that view the world with new wonderment - "What's that? Why?" And as we age our questions grow, "What's my purpose? What is this life for? What does life/God expect from me?"

Life is like beginning on the outside and as we age we work our way in; peeling away the layers like an onion with each question asked. With each new cycle or layer comes the arrival of a new awareness, a shift in perspectives that can only be achieved by, simply "living."

When our perspective shifts, the notions we ponder upon change also. One question leads to another; the more we question, the more we grow. Like the trees, the higher the tree grows, the more it can see around the obstacles that once blocked its view.

We are beings in human form seeking maturity in this garden we call Earth. As a tree matures, it bears fruit, and so it is true for humans. And when I say fruit, I'm not referring to human offspring, but the fruit of our deeds; the good each and every one of us brings to share with the world.

Knowledge is infinite, and the lessons never end. New wonderment continues to emerge, and I unearth a deeper understanding of myself and my purpose, and I am very content. It's the year 2017, and the birth of my fifty four years on planet Earth. Not only am I a storyteller, but I am a truth seeker as well.

A truth seeker is someone who reaches beyond the common wisdom of mortal men. They look within themselves for the answers that the mind questions. Some people refer to truth seekers as new age thinkers. But really, there is nothing new to seek. The knowledge is ancient. It has always been there. The only thing that is new is the awareness of it. Therefore, truth is merely a perspective. This is why one man's truth differs from another.

Many of the great spiritual teachers of the past were at the very least truth seekers: Jesus, Buddha, Rumi, and Muhammad. They all had a direct line to the heaven within – the light, the Creator, God, whatever you wish to call it; some simply call it love. Regardless, we all have this ability. Some people are born to it, while others simply need to learn the way. Still some of us choose to use it, and some do not.

After all, being a good human isn't easy. You have to be dedicated to becoming a better person in order to achieve enlightenment. But it is not impossible. If you can be truly honest with yourself, then you are halfway there. And you can trust in the fact that if you're reading this book, you too are most certainly a truth seeker.

TRUTH - Every human being struggles with the truth at one time or another. On one hand, you are humble yet huge, you feed your spirit, you are truthful, and you are aware. On the other hand you're insignificant, you're ego driven, you're dishonest, and you tend lay the blame elsewhere. These are the qualities of all humans.

> *"Why do you notice the splinter in your brother's eye, but do not perceive the wooden beam in your own eye?" Matthew 7:3*

Self-deception, is the fictitious story we tell ourselves in order to maintain a positive self image. It's a way of masking our weaknesses. To be honest with your self is a very brave act indeed. Often times it means that you stand alone. You sacrifice popularity for the greater good.

I used to think I was an honest person, until the day after I was fired from my job seven years ago. I immediately began to lay blame with my employer by focusing on her unfavorable characteristics, mainly in the form of dishonest business dealings.

Suddenly it occurred to me that I was right there with her, as an employee, when these occurrences took place. But it wasn't until she fired me that I realized that I was just as dishonest as she was.

The excuse I tried to feed myself while I was employed was, "Yeah, but it would of cost me my job if I spoke up." And I was right, but guess what, I was fired anyway. So really, I wasn't right. I was wrong all along.

This is what happened. I was working for a property management company as a property inspector. I reported to the property manager that a smoke detector was not working properly within an apartment that we managed.

The property manger failed to have the smoke detector replaced and the apartment caught on fire. The homeowner refused to take responsibility for the damage by blaming the new tenants for the damaged smoke detector. My written report, which would have held my employer responsible for the damaged smoke alarm disappeared, and my employer sided with the owner. I have no clue as to how the story played out, because I was fired soon after the incident.

But I can say this, I pulled a Pontius Pilot and washed my hands of it. Pontius Pilot, the indecisive squirrel who couldn't make up his mind as to which way to go, as a car barreled upon him in the road.

I know I'm not the only one dealing with real life situations like this. We all seek to protect ourselves and our families. No one wants to lose their job. But what message are we sending to our children when we choose to be dishonest so we may live comfortably at the expense of another? And better yet, what harm are we causing to ourselves?

Edward Snowden is a former C.I.A. (Central Intelligence Agency) agent, and former contractor for the N.S.A. (National Security Agency), who could not in good conscious continue to violate the U.S. Constitutions right to privacy.

His employers, the C.I.A. and the N.S.A. were, and most certainly still are, scanning American emails, phone calls, and they even eavesdrop through computer cameras and cell phone cameras, without a court order, or any indication of criminal activity, which is clearly a violation of the fourth amendment. Not to mention the drone assassinations that are being conducted by these agencies as well, where innocent people are being murdered, including Americans.

It's no longer a conspiracy theory; it's a fact thanks to the bravery of Edward Snowden.

Snowden made the ultimate sacrifice by releasing documents and video that supported his allegations, and is now a fugitive of the U.S. Government. He found asylum in Russia of all places. Can you imagine, Russia?

> *" . . . and I think, the greatest freedom I gained is the fact that I no longer have to worry about what happens tomorrow, because I'm happy with what I've done today." – Edward Snowden*

Yet Edward Snowden is happy. Why? Because, his conscious is clear; he didn't sit idly by in denial of his employer's behavior. He saw a wrong, and he chose to set it right. The truth will set you free! And may I add, quite literally.

There is nothing more liberating than living an honest life. One of the most liberated moments in my life was when "I stepped out of the closet." I had fallen in love with a woman, but had debated the thought for three years, before I had the nerve to pursue a relationship with her. Acknowledging that love was the happiest moment of my life; it was the bravest act that ever I endured and it set me free.

Know your truth and react accordingly. Treat other humans as you wish to be treated. If you truly want to be an honest person, then you have to live like one. If you want to change the world, change yourself – we've all heard statements such as these a thousand times, yet most of us are too busy laying blame instead of taking the time to be honest with ourselves. I have come to learn that if I am blaming another person for whatever, then I am not being honest with myself, plain and simple.

> *"A man's character determines his destiny."*

Remember, this human experience is of your creation. This is your story. You are the master of your sea. You can be a hero, or you can be the villain. It can be a stormy sea of deep depression, nothingness, black skies and death, or it can be a smooth, inviting, refreshing sea breeze kind of a story. It's easy to play the victim, yet far more rewarding if you're willing to take responsibility for who you are. Seek the truth.

There are some who seek no further than the written words in Holy books. They do not see beyond the surface at what lies beneath. You simply have to ask.

> *Jesus said, "One who seeks will find, and for one who knocks it will be opened." - Thomas 1:94*

I believe the bible to be an instructional guide on how to be human. The only drawback is that it was written so long ago that it can be a difficult to understand today. It's kind of like Shakespeare, if it wasn't for high school would any of us truly understand the symbolism within the stories?

Language is an art. I went to a wedding the other day and some kid was wearing a ball hat that said something about chopping trees, and a young lady explained to me that it meant he sold weed. I would have never guessed in a million years.

There are approximately 1,000 to 4,000 new words added to the (*English)* dictionary each year. I'm sure that someone reading this book two thousand years in the future may have some trouble understanding the message.

So here's my attempt to share what life has taught me; The Gospel of Kim, so to speak. This is my truth. This book is my fruit, my legacy of love; fish food soulfully pioneered through the magic of living.

Part I – HUMAN: THE RULES OF THE GAME

There are little decrees that apply to all human beings regardless of purpose or ones journey. Life is not meant to be complicated. A "Keep it simple stupid," approach can make for a happy ride in time.

Have you ever noticed in the old religious paintings there's this golden rounded light depicted around the heads of saints and other religious entities? And it's not just a Christian thing. You can find this golden glow in many of the paintings in other ancient religions. The halo is symbolic of a higher way of thinking. These masters discovered the power of the mind.

Evolution of the mind is the goal. The ultimate achievement of this adventure is to advance to the next level(s). To play, you must open your mind and listen from the heart. Your heart will never let you down.

Your mind on the other hand, is the seat of the ego. The ego is your free will. Without it there is no independent thinking; no choice. So you see, life really is what you create.

CHAPTER TWO - CHOICE

I am music in movement; it is I that vibrates the ocean waves and moves the wind with lightening in hand. I am human.

Be aware. Own up and realize who you are. You are powerful. Your voice and your actions, and yes, even your thoughts vibrate and shape this human reality that we share. You got skills. How you choose to use those skills is up to you, and only you.

Your greatest gift to mankind is the presence of your own awareness of this power. Once you realize how influential you are, you realize you must step softer, speak with less thunder in the mouth, with an open hand for giving and open arms for hugging.

For every action there is a reaction. This action and reaction can heal or kill. It depends on which energy you choose to generate – positive or negative?

We live in a world of twos. There's a positive and negative to everything, other than batteries. The Internet can be a good thing, but it can be a bad thing too for obvious reasons. Hurricanes can level a town, but they also bring people closer. Even herbs and foods have benefits as well as side effects, and Human's are no different.

There's an old Cherokee story that speaks of duality of human existence. It is the story of two wolves.

The grandfather tells his grandson, "The battle is between two wolves inside of us all. One is evil. It is anger, envy, jealousy, sorrow, regret, greed, arrogance, self-pity, guilt, resentment, false pride. The other is good. It is joy, peace, compassion, love, hope, serenity, humility, kindness, empathy, gratitude, generosity, and faith."

The grandson thought about it, then asked the grandfather, "Which one wins?"

The grandfather replied, "The one you feed."

> *"The right choice can be a difficult one, for it often involves sacrifice of one's pleasure."*

This constant battle inside is why we are all walking contradictions. We can all be hypocritical depending on what hat we are wearing on what day.

Therefore, nothing in this world is ever absolute. The choice to change the mind is always an option. Choice is a gift. Without it there is no freedom. This means, you are the master of your own seas.

It's your life story regardless of your environment or circumstances, you always have a choice. Every morning begins a new day, a new paragraph or a word in this chapter in your book of life. If you're unhappy, then make the choice to make the change in your life that will end the unhappiness. There is always more than one option.

> *"You can choose not to choose, but you still have made a choice." – Rush (Canadian Rock Band)*

And when we view choice from a grander scale, we can see that God did not create the chaos, we humans did that. If fluttering wings of a butterfly can create the wind, then why would it be so hard to believe that our thoughts and actions can spread, causing pain and suffering in ourselves, as well as others?

Flipping someone the bird for cutting you off at a stop light, turns into an underpaid grumpy husband on his way home from work, yelling at his kids for being child like, that in turn becomes a child bullying another at school, and it continues. Then we scratch our heads wondering why more kids are bringing guns to school.

But don't blame God for this world He created. It's the world that you and I created. Change begins by changing ourselves. And if hate can spread, so can love.

> *"There are two ways to be fooled. One is to believe what isn't true; the other is to refuse to believe what is true." – Soren Kierkegaard (Danish Philosopher & Poet)*

If you choose to open your mind and accept this belief and make a conscious effort to become more aware of your actions and the reactions of those choices, then doors will open.

But know that whichever you choose is what will serve you. Put out a good vibe and a good vibe will bounce back at you; put out some negativity, like being unforgiving, and others shall be unforgiving of you. So choose wisely.

BEGIN AGAIN

"Hi! My name is Kim, daughter of Rita, granddaughter of Katherine and Katie."

First we are born to our parents. Love them or hate them, it is said that we picked our parents before we were born. Our choice in ancestors prepares us for our journey when we begin again.

Keep in mind that our mission on Earth is to evolve and grow. So resistance is a natural occurrence; meaning we didn't necessarily pick our parents because they are the most supporting and loving personalities.

In order to expand we have to go against the grain so to speak. The bible story of the Wedding at Cana depicts a pushy mother and a mouthy son, from a human perspective. It also marks the *beginning* of Jesus' ministry, as he turns water into wine.

It is somewhat symbolic that as Jesus begins his adult life, he turns water, of all things, into wine.

All four of the Gospels begin with birth and baptism (water). Water is very significant in regards to evolution. I'm not saying that man evolved from apes, but we most certainly came from water. Human fetuses in the early stage of development have gill slits; we're surrounded by water while we're in our mother's womb; and if you are Catholic, then you most likely were baptized in water soon after your birth. Water is symbolic of birth and blessings.

We are basically made of water. Some body parts contain more water than others. Water connects us. Look at the ocean or gaze over the Great Lakes, or a river or stream and tell me where does the water begin and where does it end?

There's water in the air, it transfers up and down; sometimes there is more water in the air than other times, but it's always there.

Water is life. As Yoko Ono put it, "You are water, I'm water; we're all water in different containers. That's why it's so easy to meet. Someday we'll evaporate together."

> *"If in thirst you drink water from a cup, you see God in it. Those not in love with God only see their face in it." – Rumi (Persian Sunni Muslim Poet)*

And if you haven't noticed yet, the more polluted our waters become, the more toxic our society has become. Or maybe we ought to examine that statement from another perspective; the more polluted the minds of society has become the dirtier the water.

A Japanese Doctor of Alternative Medicine named Masaru Emoto has proven the impact our thoughts can have on water, as well as each other. Dr. Emoto began by studying water crystals. He attached words to the water and then took note of how the water crystallized.

~ Water Yourself Daily ~

Words like love and gratitude crystallized beautifully; brilliant attractive shapes, in contrast to words such as hate and even the name Hitler. The negative words crystallized into dull and distorted shapes.

To further his theory, Emoto gathered a group of monks and asked that they pray over a polluted body of water with the intention of healing the water and clearing it of toxins. For one hour a hundred or so people meditated. The water was then tested afterwards, and found to have improved. Once again proving that thought has a profound effect on water.

Considering our bodies contain up to ninety percent water, it can be concluded that our thoughts have a direct impact on our bodies, as well as influencing those we come in contact with.

Emoto's research demonstrates that water holds memory. This is where an awareness of power comes in play, an understanding of how our actions can hurt or heal.

Just as words have an effect on the water, the moon has an effect on the waters tide. Again the same can be said in regards to the human body. Human emotions are known to run high on a full moon, and water has historically been known to symbolize emotions.

New beliefs are emerging in the medical field linking behavior with disease. The metaphysics of mind body health, backed by quantum mechanics. Just like climate change though, some will believe and others will doubt the correlation, regardless of the science. And still, it does not change the reality that our words and actions vibrate and ripple affecting all.

> *"Be like water making its way through cracks. Do not be assertive, but adjust to the object, and you shall find a way round or through it. If nothing in you stays rigid, outward things will disclose themselves. Empty your mind, be formless." – Bruce Lee (Martial Arts Instructor & Philosopher)*

Water is sacred. There's no doubt about it. With knowledge comes responsibility. Once you know something, you can not UN-know it. Either you accept the responsibility and live it, or you do not. There may be times when you do and times when you don't. Regardless, the choice is always available, as well as the opportunity to begin again.

EYE BELIEVE!

Seeing is believing. Yet we believe in radio waves; they are unseen. And have you ever wondered why a ninety-year old who drinks, swears and smokes like a chimney is still here among us cancer free?

Take for instance Keith Richards of the Rolling Stones. That man has partied and smoked all his life, yet he has outlived the most cautious of us all. Which in turn goes to show that what you believe can save you or kill you.

We all have a choice as to what to believe.

When I was a child, in the early 70's, my mother tried to tell me that white people and black people do not date each other; that we were separate. At the time of this conversation, I had just pointed out a dark skinned boy I had a crush on, whom I had shared a ride home with on the Catholic school bus.

So I said to her, "Jesus says we're all the same. 'They are red and yellow, black and white they are precious in His sight.'"

Her comeback, "Didn't Jesus say to obey your parents?"

What could I say? She had a point.

A couple of years later and my mom and dad divorced. Back then divorce was unheard of, and suddenly I was different from my classmates, and I was told that my mom and dad would no longer be able to participate in the Holy Sacrament of Communion.

So I said to my teacher, "Doesn't Jesus say to forgive?" I did not understand why Jesus would not allow my parents to participate in Church activities simply because they no longer wanted to live together. It made no sense to me as a child, and it is still meaningless to me today.

> *"Truly I say to you, unless you turn and become like little children, you shall never enter the kingdom of heaven." - Matthew 18-3*

Lessons in hypocrisy learned early on. Life is like being born into the Old Testament and maturing into the new. We take on the old beliefs of our parents and others whom have impacted our lives. And as we grow life events will challenge those beliefs.

When I was twelve or thirteen years of age, I came close to drowning. It's true what they say; the third time down is the last. And as I went down the third time, my life flashed before my eyes and a calm came over me, and I saw Jesus above me with his is arms stretched out, and an angel on both sides kneeling near His feet.

I'll never forget it, but as I grew older and become more cynical of the world, I began to question what I had seen. Like, "I bet I saw that picture somewhere when I was in Catholic school, and that it was all a figment of my childish imagination."

Yet, I could never explain away the calmness that came upon me. There was no fear; just warmth and peace and an understanding that death isn't such a bad thing. If anything, it was somewhat inviting.

Fast forward to age twenty three - I've left my home and family approximately 2,000 miles to the East. I'm living in Southern California, and had been hanging out at the pool all day. I regularly wear a St. Christopher medallion that my mother had given me as a gift, but I had taken it off to avoid a tan line.

It's a beautiful day and the sun is about to set. So I hop on my bike (motorcycle), with my head in the clouds, and I totally forget to put my St. Christopher necklace back on. I could have turned around and retrieved it, but I didn't. Instead I began questioning the existence of such an entity as I pushed forward to get some beer at the corner store.

As I approached the store, I had the sun at my back not realizing that the sun was blinding to those who were driving into it. Before I knew it, a pickup truck was turning in front of me across my path. He couldn't see me!

He hit me on my left side pinching my pinkie finger against the handlebar grip, and catching my hip and breaking the rear left turn signal. I miraculously kept the bike up on two wheels and came to a wobbly stop. I walked away with nothing more than a bruised finger and hip. Some would say I'm lucky, but the truth is I'm blessed.

> *"I don't believe, I know." – Carl Jung (Psychoanalyst)*

I no longer wear the St. Christopher medallion on a daily basis, but I do know that St. Christopher is real in my world. I speak to him all the time. Especially if I see a stray animal running loose. I ask St. Christopher to protect that lost pet on its journey, and I ask St. Francis to talk to the animal and tell it to go home and stay out of the street. Then I thank them both. And I can honestly say that I have never seen a pet that I have prayed for on the road later, dead.

Life's lessons – the stronger the belief, the more effective it becomes. The down side to that statement is that it makes it just as hard to change a belief that no longer serves you.

To believe or not to believe; it is a choice. If you choose to see those little miracles for what they are, life becomes a more magical. And the same can be said when we release a self serving belief, like those defensive walls we all put up to keep us sheltered from the hurt and anger.

> *"Your task is not to seek for love, but merely to seek and find all the barriers within yourself that you have built against it." - Rumi*

To rediscover ourselves, we must tear the walls of doubt from our minds, and we begin by training our minds to flow on a positive note. Daily affirmations are short positive declarations intended to change or affirm a belief. Examples would include (by Louise Hay):

- I begin the day with a song.
- I am full of praise and gratitude.
- I am a magnet for joy; you are a magnet for joy.
- Everyday is fun for me; everyday is fun for you.
- My arms are made for hugging; your arms are made for hugging; I love to hug!

Repeat an affirmation often and eventually the subconscious mind will accept that affirmation as truth. You can buy books full of affirmations. Or you can look up Louise Hay on YouTube and play hours of affirmations for free. I know it might sound silly, but listen to Louise as part of your morning routine, and I guarantee you'll feel better about yourself.

You can create your own affirmations, and write them out on little post it notes and stick them to the mirror or on the wall near the coffee pot, anywhere where you can see them often. Simply keep your statements positive and avoid negative words.

My wife kept telling me she was fat, so I wrote this affirmation, "I'm not fat, I'm fantastic!" And then I stuck it to the bathroom mirror where she could see it daily.

If you can think yourself into it,

you can think yourself out of it!

One of the greatest scientific minds in time, Albert Einstein, a German-American theoretical physicist and founder of the theory of relativity said, "A true sign of intelligence is not knowledge but imagination. Logic will get you from point A to B. Imagination will take you everywhere."

A strange thought for a scientist you would think, but Einstein wasn't your typical scientist. Just today as I am writing this, "Albert Einstein's weirdest prediction that the universe is sprinkled with massive objects so dense that not even light can escape them," is in the news tonight (NBC News – April 5, 2017, Earth Sized Telescope May Let Us See A Black Hole For The First Time Ever).

The smartest man in the world also said, "There are only two ways to live your life. One is as though nothing is a miracle; the other is as though everything is a miracle."

Another scientist, Bruce Lipton, PhD, a cell biologist and author of, "The Biology of Belief (2008)," explains how the body is a product of the mind. He explains how positive thoughts can keep you healthy, and that bad or negative thoughts will bring sickness and disease to the body. Lipton uses an example of the nocebo effect (opposite of the placebo effect) to show how the body reacts to the mind.

In 1974, Nashville physician, Clifton Meador had a patient named Sam Londe, who was a retired salesman with esophagus cancer. The disease is considered fatal. Londe ended up dying about three weeks later. At the time of the autopsy, only a small amount of cancer was found in Londe's body; there was a spot on his lung and one on his liver, but not enough to kill him.

What's really mind blowing was there was no esophagus cancer of any kind. Three decades later and Dr. Meador is still haunted by Londe's death. Meador told the Discovery Channel, "He died with cancer, but not from cancer. I thought he had cancer, he thought he had cancer, everyone around him thought he had cancer . . . did I remove hope in some way?"

Lipton goes on and shares another mind blowing experience in his book, "The Biology of Belief." Published in the New England Journal of Medicine, in 2002, a study led by Dr. Bruce Moseley, of Baylor School of Medicine, divided his knee surgery patients into three groups. In the first group, Moseley shaved the damage cartilage in the knee. The second group, Moseley simply flushed the knee joint. And in the third group, he conducted a fake surgery.

The "fake surgery" patients were sedated, and the standard incisions were made; he splashed water to stimulate the sound of the knee washing and talked and acted like he would, if he had truly done the surgery. All three groups were given the same post surgery instructions.

The placebo group improved right along with the first two groups. Lipton quotes Moseley as saying, "My skill as a surgeon had no benefit on these patients. The entire benefit of surgery for osteoarthritis of the knee was the placebo effect."

This isn't opinion, its science. You are the Captain of your ship; your body. That is if you choose to believe and are willing to take on the responsibility. If so, then its time to break free and sprout!

THE MIND

The mind is a powerful tool, more powerful than most of us are aware of. I don't think it ever sleeps. Millions of thoughts pass through our minds daily. I have even found myself with jibber jabber thoughts racing through my head as I slowly awaken in the morning.

One day on my morning commute, a girl in a van cut me off three times. After the third time, I had some choice words for her, or I guess I should say some choice thoughts. But at the time, I was taking metaphysical classes, and I reminded myself to change my thoughts into something more positive. So I thought to myself, "I'm sorry sister, I didn't mean to call you a witch. Please forgive me."

At the next light we pull up beside each other, and the young lady rolled her window down and motioned me to do the same. She then said, "I am so sorry for cutting you off. I'm in a hurry. Please forgive me."

That made my day! Oh my God, I was floored. I couldn't wipe the smile from my face. Wow!

You only need to believe it to be true for it happen to you too. I do this every time I get stopped for a speeding ticket now. I simply send good thoughts towards the officer that pulled me over.

I think things like, "Oh, you're having a great day! It's a happy day. I love you brother (or sister). I wish you the best. You don't want to give me a ticket." And I kid you not, it works.

Try it on your spouse or a co-worker who's having a bad day.

What we think of others has an impact on them. That's why it is really important to be aware of the thoughts that are running through our minds. What you think is what you will get.

Back in the day, if I was to be pulled over, my first thoughts would have been, "Damn, another ticket." Then I would find a way to justify my position and lay blame with the cop, whether I was speeding or not. And I got a ticket every time. My thoughts were leading me to an outcome in which I would get ticketed. It's kind of like looking in a mirror. What you say, do, think or feel will reflect back at you.

My wife and I recently took a trip to Southern California. We reserved a 4 x 4 as car rental, but ended up with a minivan. What was even a bigger disappointment was that it came with Alabama tags. My first thought was, "Great! People are going to think we're a couple of racist bible thumpers traveling with two pit bulls (we took our dogs with us)."

So we arrive in California, and I'm ecstatic because I just love the Mexican food found in San Diego. It's like no other that is served here in the States. I had lived there years ago, and fell in love with the Mexican culture as well.

So the wife and I stumbled upon a small Mexican restaurant not far from the beach. My wife ordered two beef tacos, and I had ordered two carne asada (steak) tacos, and I ordered a pineapple drink. The wife ate one of my tacos and I ate one of her tacos, and I took three sips of the drink that I had ordered. My wife had nothing to drink.

The reason I only took three sips of that delicious pineapple drink was because I had become suspicious when our hostess took my cup into the back of the kitchen while making sure the double swinging doors behind her were shut completely. Then she brought my glass back out and placed ice in the cup and then filled it with the pineapple juice.

Within five minutes of leaving the two tabled Mexican taco shop, my stomach was cramping and I had to use the toilet bad! Like right now! My wife, who didn't touch the drink at all, was fine.

Although the truth is unknown to me as to why this young Mexican girl put something in my drink, I couldn't help but feel that I had become in her eyes the very thing I thought and felt about people in Alabama.

I wasn't rude to the young woman. I do not know her. I believe it was racist gesture on her part, created by my own intolerant thoughts of Southern white people in general.

Knowing what I know about thought, I am sure I'm the one who placed me in that position. Therefore, the blame lies within me.

If you would like to test the waters, try this.

Before you pull into a Wal-Mart parking lot, or the grocery lot, tell yourself there is a front row parking space there for you and you alone. Say it to yourself as if you truly believe it. You have to really want it and trust it to be true in order for it to manifest. If it doesn't work the first time, remove the doubt and try again.

DOUBT

To doubt is to fear or suspect, mistrust or to question the truth of. The opposite of doubt would be faith. True faith leaves no room for doubt.

We all have our dark moments, no matter how enlightened we may become. Pope John Paul II and Mother Theresa have both stated that they had their moments of doubt.

Jesus said, "Truly, I say to you, if you have and do not doubt, you will not only do what has been done to the fig tree, but even if you say to this mountain, 'Be taken up and thrown into the sea,' it will happen." (Mathew 21:21)

Muhammad Ali, champion boxer, activist, and a student of the Islamic religion nails it on the head when he said, "It isn't the mountains ahead to climb that wear you out; it's the pebble in your shoe."

In other words, it is the doubt that robs you of your energy. It surrenders power and says, "I cannot do it." It's an emotional response to fear; it is a product of the thoughts you create; it is a choice.

You wouldn't run with a pebble in your shoe, then why would you live with doubt in your mind?

There is a saying that only those who believe in magic will know magic; those who do not believe will never know the magic that exists in the human life.

> *"But he should ask in faith, not doubting, for the one who doubts is like a wave of the sea that is driven and tossed about by the wind," James 1:6*

Faith moves mountains. And it begins by having faith in you, yourself. The kingdom of Heaven is within you. Heaven resides in every human being, no matter who you are. Even though some people may appear to shine brighter than others, we all are of the same light and judgment is not allowed.

> "Our deepest fear is not that we are inadequate. Our deepest fear is that we are powerful beyond measure. It is our light, not our darkness that most frightens us. We ask ourselves, "Who am I to be brilliant, gorgeous, talented, fabulous? Actually, who are you not to be? You are a child of God. Your playing small does not serve the world. There is nothing enlightened about shrinking so that other people won't feel insecure around you. We are all meant to shine, as children do. We were born to make manifest the glory of God within us. It's not just some of us; it's in everyone. And as we let our own light shine, we unconsciously give other people permission to do the same. As we are liberated from our own fear, our presence automatically liberates others." – Marianne Williamson (Author of A Return to Love)

Sometimes I find myself doubting my capabilities as a writer.

Am I wasting my time on this book? Should I get a regular job with a regular paycheck? Does anyone really care about what I have to share with the world?

Yet I strive and I continue to write and shape this book because I have faith in who I am. I choose to ignore the doubt that pulls at my mind. I was born with a gift, and I choose to share that gift with the world.

"Just as from the heavens the rain and snow came down and do not return there till they have watered the earth, making it fertile and fruitful, giving seed to the one who sows and bread to the one who eats, so shall my word be that goes forth from my mouth: it shall not return to me void, but shall do my will, achieving the end for which I sent for it," Isaiah 55:10-11.

Regardless of what others say, or if I only sell ten copies of this book, I know that I gave it my best. And that in itself is success.

So I pull that pebble from my shoe, and I keep running up that mountain. We all have a purpose, and we all have a gift to share. Pluck the doubt from your mind, and feel the purpose in your heart.

CHAPTER THREE - CHANGE

Like I said earlier, nothing of this human experience stays the same – nothing. Nothing in this reality is absolute, other than our time on this Earth plain is limited – we all die. Everything changes all the time, everyday. With every sunrise comes a new day, a new opportunity to move, to create, to change who we are. If yesterday was a bad day, you can switch direction on the winds of change tomorrow. No exceptions; this is true for all humans.

The sad side to this spectacular benefit of life is that sometimes people we love leave us. Not just in death, but lovers break apart, friends relocate to the far reaches on a map. Or grief can come with the loss of a job.

For many of us, when we are confronted with change, we automatically kick into fear mode, and begin sabotaging ourselves from the word go. We say things like, "This won't work. I can't do it. It's impossible!"

Remember to remove the doubt from the mind. Stand confident and trust that you'll be ok. Trust isn't only the foundation of good healthy and hearty relationships, it powers belief.

There will be times when a belief will be challenged and tested. Maybe that belief needs strengthened. Or maybe the circumstances surrounding a particular belief have changed. There are many perspectives in which to view a belief. Soul evolution is all about change, and emotions ensure an ever changing adventure, trust me.

When I lived in Southern California, in the mid 80's, drivers were shooting other drivers who were moving too slow, or who may have pulled out in front of the shooter. It was pretty much the birth of road rage as I knew it.

So I began to carry a pistol in my pick-up truck for protection. One day this guy in front of me at an intersection blew off our green light to allow traffic from the other direction to turn in front of us. It was a hot summer day in afternoon rush hour traffic. Maybe he thought he was doing a good thing. Yet he didn't have any concern for those of us behind him, who sat through two lights.

I beeped my horn in frustration. Who knows, maybe he had fallen asleep? I'd say maybe he was having car problems, but his foot never left the brake. Anyway, he gets out of his car with an angry look on his face, and I flash him my pistol. It didn't take him long to get back in his truck. He drove on when that light turned green a third time.

I was angry and that was the last time I ever carried a gun. If that man hadn't gotten back in his car, I may have shot him. Or who knows, maybe he would have pulled a gun on me. Either way, I had become the person whom I was protecting myself from.

Change – said the man in the mirror; so I changed. No more weapons of destruction. I made a choice to use my hands for loving and healing instead.

If the ride gets rough, and you are feeling stuck and down on your luck, it is an indication of resistance to change. Life is meant to flow like water, or music.

> *"Strictly speaking, they did not find God through their suffering, because suffering implies resistance. They found God through surrender, through total acceptance of what is, into which they were forced by their intense suffering."*
> *– Eckhart Tolle, Author of The Power of Now*

If it's out of your hands; you cannot change it, simply accept it and say yes to what is. Have faith that this happening has a reason. Who knows, maybe because that man sat through two lights it kept me from becoming involved in a deadly car accident.

If you're feeling stuck or depressed you may want to consider changing your routine. In the past fifteen years I've started my day by watching the news and working out in my home in the morning, to beginning my day on social media, to beginning the day praying the rosary and feeding my mind new information in regards to worldwide beliefs and spiritual healing. A change in routine has the power to spark new life.

Whether we like it or not, the universe will nudge us onto the next lesson. After all, it's written in the stars.

It is said that at one time numerology and astrology were part of the bible, which really isn't as farfetched as it sounds, when you consider the bible contains a chapter called Numbers and there is at least forty-one or more bible verses that refer to the stars, sun and moon.

The stars have traditionally been the focus of many cultures through out the ages. And we know that the moon not only affects the ocean tides, but also us human beings due to our connectedness to the water; at the very least, common sense dictates that the science of astrology is most certainly worthy of deliberation when considering the forces (like the moon) that influence our Earthly existence.

So face it – change is a part of life on Earth. There really is no way of avoiding it, but how you react to uncertainty can make the world a better place or a worse place.

Bounce back from the shock and spring into action. Be resilient and flow with what you are handed. Keep your focus; keep your faith. Control your thoughts. Keep an optimistic perspective.

So you lost your job, instead of freaking out on how you're going to pay the bills, maybe change your thoughts to those of excitement and wonderment – "I wonder what kind job the universe has in store for me next?"

If you look forward to your new adventure, the smoother the transition, but if you dread the change and feed your mind doubt, then you will surely struggle.

> *"You never change things by fighting the existing reality. To change something, build a new model that makes the existing model obsolete." - Buckminster Fuller (American Architect & Inventor)*

Use (Louise Hay) affirmations like - the perfect job is looking for me, and we are being brought together now; I have unlimited potential, only good lies before me; I have the perfect job, It is wonderful work, with wonderful pay; getting a job was easy. Repeat the affirmations daily, as if they are true happenings. And close your eyes and visualize that new job.

Creative Visualization is the process of creating a mental image with the intent to generate a realistic outcome. Creative visualization has gained massive popularity among athletes of all kinds. Before a game some athletes will visualize that touchdown pass, or that half court shot. They see it playing out in their mind, up to a hundred times, or more. They visualize it, they feel it, and then they play it just as they saw it in their minds eye.

There was a man named Viktor Frankl, who survived the Nazi concentration camps of World War II, by visualizing himself lecturing after the war and dreaming of seeing his wife again. He survived and wrote a bestselling book called, "Man's Search For Meaning."

If you have surgery, you can use creative visualization as tool to help you heal. Visualize the injured part of your body healing.

See yourself getting stronger. Use your affirmations as well – "I feel good; my body heals with the passing of each day."

And if you're dealing with that dreaded change that comes in the form of loss, then it's going to take some time. There is no overnight fix for a broken heart. Still, every bit of this advice will help you on your healing journey. It's true what they say, "When one door closes, another opens." Have faith, and believe.

MUSIC & COLOR

Ancient medicine and modern science both agree that life is formed from vibration. This includes tone and light. Both music and color transcend barriers universally and have a direct and immediate effect on the human body. Both music and color stimulate and activate the entire brain, in addition to feeding the spirit and the ability to heal. Incorporate the two to any healing experience and you have a holistic fix for sure, and you don't have to be a guru to do it. Simply shut the world out, close your eyes and turn the music up and visualize.

Music eases stress and depression. That's why bars have juke boxes. Whether you're celebrating or feeling sorry for yourself, alcohol and music just seem to go together. This doesn't mean you have to drink to feel the highs and lows of the songs we live.

Music can cure things that medication never will. The human heart is a rhythm machine pumping blood. There is no cell in your body that is not affected by vibration.

Before the music we know today, there was the drum. Everything in the universe vibrates to sound. Drumming is a natural way of energizing and removing energy blocks from within the body. Drumming opens the heart to a higher vibration and the mind to worlds unseen. It's an excellent healing experience.

Shaman's often listen to rhythmic percussion as a way to carry the soul into a nonconventional reality, or a parallel universe so to speak. On these journeys a shaman can gather information from spirit guides to aid patients or the community.

We all have spirit guides. It's a method that any one today can use to get answers to personal questions. The fact that the practice has been around for thousands of years is a testament to the capabilities of the method.

Sandra Ingerman has written a few books in regards to shamanic journeying, including a beginner's guide that comes with a drumming CD.

Other alternatives include drum circles. When we come together in a circle everybody contributes freely a unique perspective in the form of sound and movement. It becomes a shared energy that creates an attractive sound and feel. After a few hours of drumming into the night, I sleep good, and in the morning I awake feeling vibrant and renewed.

If you are unable hook up with a drum circle, which I highly recommend if you want to amplify the drumming experience, then find some music that you would like to drum to and play along with it. You are a walking vibration, so know that everyone and anyone can drum. Don't feed the doubt – you CAN do it!

> CAUTION: Music may cause sudden outburst of joy and spontaneous healing.

What you listen to throughout your day will have an impact on how you feel. Dis-ease is disharmony. Self destructive music will not lead you to the road to salvation. So use a little caution as to what you choose to listen to. Focus and listen to your body. Your body will tell you if a song *feels* good or not. The same is true for color.

Color is a property of light that is broken down into different frequencies. The Chinese have traditionally used color as way to harmonize with the surrounding environment; this ancient art of placement is called Feng Shui. Translated, feng shui means wind-water, and is one of the Five Arts of Chinese Metaphysics.

Take for instance the color green, feng shui says green symbolizes growth and harmony and is considered restful and refreshing. The color is good to use in therapy rooms and bathrooms, but not in studies, family rooms or playrooms.

Blue on the other hand is peaceful and linked to spirituality, contemplation and patience. Blue promotes trust and stability, or can be melancholia and promote suspicion; its suggested use is for meditation rooms, bathrooms and rooms used for therapy, but not in family rooms, studies or dining rooms.

Purple is great for bedrooms and meditation rooms, but not in bathrooms or kitchens.

> *Ying is the blackness that absorbs color – Yang is the whiteness that reflects color.*

Hinduism/Buddhism on the other hand, has used color throughout the ages to heal and restore energy within the human body, often referred to as the chakras system. The word Chakra translates into circles, wheel, and/or cycle. Chakras are implied positions along the spine where the universal life force is contained within the body.

There are seven chakra's within the body beginning at the root chakra located at the tailbone; its color is red. The next chakra is the spleen chakra and its color is orange; the solar plexus chakra is yellow; the heart chakra green; the throat chakra is blue; the third eye or brow chakra is indigo; and the crown chakra is violet.

Say you have a friend who was hospitalized due to a major heart attack, you may want to contribute to your friends healing by visualizing the color green surrounding your loved one (never use the green for cancer patients with tumors; green is the color of growth).

Or if you are having problems related to the kidneys or bladder, you may want to consider visualizing the color orange; maybe wear an orange shirt, or carry an orange gem stone in your pocket.

You can find guided chakra meditations on YouTube. Just be sure to try a few to get a feel for what makes you feel your best. Some are better than others.

Music and color can change your day, mood or moment; no doubt about it! There's no getting around color, it's in the landscape, our hair, and even the leaves in the trees change color as the season's cycle. Fashion dictates that we wear earth colors in the fall and pastels in the spring.

Even factories and successful corporate offices across America use color to influence their employees and their consumers. Color is a major marketing tool used by executives looking to hook you into purchasing their product. The mind control often comes in the form of color beaming into your living room via television. And it isn't just a product for sale, but a way of servicing your head.

Remember the power that repetitive messages can have on your subconscious. Be aware of those outside influences that strive to shape the mind. Whether it's a T.V. commercial or the nightly news, it is another outside influence that shapes and molds our reality.

WIRED TO CONNECT

All humans are wired to connect. It's clearly a natural human condition. We have radio, television, phones and now the Internet.

Ah, the Internet. Native American prophecies spoke of a giant spider web that would encompass the world one day. So here we are.

The spider is a master weaver and considered the guardian of the ancient alphabet/language. Humanity has spun its web, and as we connect and open our hearts, we share our sacredness with each other, and a new understanding is born; a new perspective. We are becoming citizens of the planet, instead of citizens of a flag. It truly is a very exciting time to be alive!

If connecting with others physically would be as simple as accepting friend request on a social media site, the human world would be so less lonely. How many people do you cross paths with physically within a day without making eye contact?

Mother Teresa use to tell the sisters to greet everyone they come in contact with throughout the day with a smile. And they did. They lived their belief. They reached beyond their comfort zone and made a connection. So you see it really isn't as hard as we like to make it out to be.

> *"Actions are the seed of fate; deeds grow into destiny" – Jean Nidetch (Founder of Weight Watchers)*

When I smile and say hi to a stranger and they smile back, my heart swells ten sizes and my smile widens even more. We all have this ability to lift each other high, and make the world a better place and there is nothing hard about it. It simply begins with a smile followed by a wave of the hand, and ta-da, we have planted seeds of love. You want to take it a step further, hug a stranger; a homeless person could most certainly use a hug.

Never think you're better than another human being. Disconnecting is division. You not only divide yourself from others, you disconnect from love; the light; the source, God (whatever name you choose to use), it's the thing that connects us.

We are merely fragments of that which is greater than ourselves. When we cause harm to another, we cause harm to ourselves. That's why it feels so good when we smile and hug. To lift the heart of another human, or any living being, is the greatest gift you can give to another, including yourself.

> *"Yesterday I was cleaver, so I wanted to change the world. Today I am wise, so I am changing myself." – Rumi (Persian Sunni Muslim Poet)*

When we change perspectives, we change the experience. Even pain and illness can be viewed as blessings.

In December of 2014, I found myself in the hospital emergency room with a white blood cell count so high that the doctors could not believe that I was able to talk and make sense at the same time. It turned out to be one of those near death experiences that forced me into relying upon other people for everything. I had to relinquish control. I had to connect with people that otherwise I would never have spoken to.

When I was finally able to use the bathroom, they put a porta-pot right by my bed, because I was too weak to walk anywhere. I had to have a nurse help me out of bed so I could pee and clean me when I was done!

Talk about humility. It most certainly was a very humbling experience. I was forced into a position where I had to trust other human beings; trust the universe and go along with the ride. No resistance; just naked; stripped of my ego.

> *"Death is a stripping away of all that is not you. The secret of life is to "die before you die" – and find that there is no death." - Eckhart Tolle*

If you want to see the better side of humanity, go to a hospital. It is said that hospitals walls have heard more prayers than church walls.

I swear the love in my heart grew enormously as the walls I had built to protect it melted away. I suddenly found myself wanting to help people. That's all I wanted do. I couldn't wait to get stronger so I could be of service to others. This book is a result of that struggle. I want to touch as many lives as I can. I want to share my happiness. If I could, I would climb from these pages and hug you right now.

Today I say yes way more than no.

Change is like a tidal wave. It is a powerful force. No matter how dramatic or sad, there is grace in every twist and turn. Roll with it; don't panic. No fear! Fear is nothing more than an emotion; a product of the mind; it is not real. You have a choice to feed the fear or defy it.

And no, I am not saying to go out today and do something dangerous that could quite possibly get you killed. The kind of fear I'm talking about is the one that keeps us from reaching our full potential; the one that keeps us disconnected, afraid and suspicious of each other.

What I'm saying is today when you step outside of your cave that you make a commitment to make eye contact with every person who crosses your path and smile and say hello. Be brave and say it like you mean it, straight from the heart. Connect. Be generous and give someone the benefit of the doubt; perform an anonymous good deed, buy a homeless person a meal, or volunteer at a hospital or convalescent home. It'll make you high, it will relieve stress and depression, and according to research you'll live longer.

> *"We were all humans until race disconnected us, religion separated us, politics divided us and wealth classified us."*
> *- Anonymous*

You have the power to control your thoughts. Don't allow race to disconnect you from us. Don't allow religion to separate you from us. Don't allow politics to divide us and classify us.

PURPOSE & PASSION

Passion is like fuel for humans. It's a natural enthusiastic and compelling feeling of love (or extreme lack of) and attraction. It is a blast of heart-felt emotional energy focused on a person, place, thought, idea, subject or thing. Passion is pure desire that compels us to evolve.

When the Deepwater Horizon exploded in the Gulf of Mexico (notoriously known as the BP Oil Spill), it had a very negative environmental impact on my home here in Pensacola, Florida. It tore my heart apart and motivated me to make a change.

The devastation ignited a passion to protect the ocean waters. I protested and led protests, and I wrote a book called, The Crude Oil Adventure of the Human Re-Evolution.

Protesting and writing (action) took me from a deep depression to one of hope. I became aware of a deeper relationship to the Earth. To harm the Earth or other creatures is to harm ourselves as well.

I used to kill bugs I found in my house. Now I will make an attempt to capture them and take them back outside, before I'll kill one. This requires some bravery when it includes palmetto bugs (3" flying cockroaches). But most of the time, I have found that the bug is just as scared of me as I once was of it. I don't want to be the bug's monster; I don't want to be anyone's monster. So another wall of fear falls.

> *"Fear is the prison walls that surround the heart."*

That's how passion works. It motivates and turns your head all around. I'm now much more aware of my purpose on this earth, and it is not to destroy, but to live in harmony with nature.

Five years after the oil spill, I found myself in the hospital in a bad way. My passion then shifted to healing myself. I became much more aware of my body and began speaking to the areas of my body that were in distress. This in turn led to a deeper understanding of the universes that exist inside of us. Love yourself and be good to yourself.

My passion led me to my purpose and as I heal myself, I share what I learn within my community. Once a month I publish a newsletter and pass it out at the Farmer's Market, as well as in hospital waiting rooms, and other public places. It's called, "The Holistic Fix," and it contains information in regards to healing physically, mentally, and spiritually. Pretty much like this book, but with herbal remedies included. The purpose of the newsletter is to bring hope to those who are feeling hopelessness.

Life isn't just about helping people, but being of service to others. Regardless of who you are we all have a purpose. Purpose is reason. We were created for a reason.

Feel your passion and find a way to apply it so that others benefit from it and you too will prosper. And even if your passion doesn't lead you to the big payday payoff, remember that what we do in this world reflects in the spirit world, and karma can be a good thing too; it's not restricted to negative behavior. Lucky people are lucky for a reason.

CHAPTER FOUR – A RECIPIE FOR HAPPINESS

Happiness is a lot of things to a lot of different people. Here in the United States we have this crazy idea that the more we consume the happier we'll be, yet suicide is the tenth leading cause of death in the good old U.S. of A. The New York Times reported, in April 2016, that suicide rates have been rising by 2% per year, since 2006.

We can plug our ears all we want, but true happiness begins with being happy with what we have; often referred to as **gratitude**.

After 9/11 I decided to sell my house in Columbus, Ohio and move to Florida. I gave myself a month to find a new house and make the move, after the deal closed on my Ohio home. When I made the first trip south to find a house to buy, I went to the beach and collected a bunch of small white shells and honored my angel for protecting me on my journey. So when I looked at a house with a flower bed full of white shells by the front door, I knew that I had found the perfect home.

> *"Gratitude unlocks the fullness of life. It turns what we have into enough, and more. It can turn a meal into a feast, a house into a home, a stranger into a friend." – Melody Beattie (American Author)*

There are four beautiful live oak trees in the yard of my new home. When Hurricane Ivan came in September 2004, there wasn't a leaf left in any of those trees and many massive branches, taller than the house itself, littered the lawn, but the house was untouched. Again I honored my angel, except this time I used the wood that had fallen from the trees.

When we create something out of love to honor a blessing or an event, it reflects brightly in the spirit world. It is an expression of appreciation.

Gratitude can also shape the mind into a positive force. When I quit smoking, or if I get a craving for a cigarette, I close my eyes and say, "I want for nothing. At this moment I need nothing. I have all I need." - Magic words indeed.

Without gratitude there is no successful marriage. Want to do well in life? Recognize those daily blessings and give thanks. It can be as easy as saying thank you. "Thank you, and bless all those who make it possible for this food to be upon our table tonight; especially to the one who prepared it. Amen."

When you develop a thankful perspective you'll find that your plate is always full. The older you get the more you will realize that you will always have what you need to survive. The only threat to your livelihood is that fear of never having enough.

A good example would be how some Americans have become fearful of the Mexican people. It is a fearful man who will stand at an imaginary line in the sand with a sign in his hand telling his brothers and sisters to the South that they are unwanted and less entitled than he himself.

Be grateful for what you have, because we're talking about people who are so desperately poor that they choose to endure a life threatening journey just to get here to America. Most are passionate hearts, with only a dream as their guide, which is why they call America the home of the brave.

The next ingredient to a life of happiness is **forgiveness.** No matter how angry or wronged you may feel you must release the pain; let go so that you may continue to flow freely without struggle.

> *"For every minute you are angry, you lose 60 seconds of happiness." – Ralph Waldo Emerson (American Philosopher and Poet)*

When we refuse to forgive someone and we hold onto that hurt, it in turn decreases the love we are generating. It's like hanging a heavy wet towel on your shoulders. It feels heavy and weighs you down, except it is our spirit that carries the weight when we do not forgive others. We have to release the hurt. Otherwise it can show up as disease within the body.

> *"The weak can never forgive. Forgiveness is an attribute of the strong." – Mahatma Gandhi*

There's an ancient Hawaiian practice called Ho'oponopono, which means, "to make right." You create a mental picture of the person you need to forgive in your mind, and from your heart you say, "I am sorry, please forgive me, thank you, I love you."

You can repeat this in any order. You don't even have to talk directly to the person who caused you pain, but you can forgive them in your mind and in your heart.

And while we are forgiving those with whom we interact, we can also practice Ho'oponopono when we see a shooter on the nightly news, who takes out a movie theater, because we need to take responsibility for our actions.

Face it, we can all be assholes at one time or another and for every action there is a reaction (it spreads). And if our negativity spreads, then we most certainly need to ask for forgiveness due to those actions contributing to that shooter's state of mind, on the nightly news. Of course we can all ask for forgiveness from the victims as well, since we did contributed to that hurt and anger that caused their deaths.

I'm sorry

Please forgive me

Thank you

I love you

The total world is of your creation. Ho'oponopono is taking total responsibility for your life; if it's in your life, then it is your responsibility.

Plus, being human and second chances go hand in hand; there is no such thing as the perfect person. Our perfection is in being imperfect. Without imperfection we would be rather boring, wouldn't you think? Kind of like a well-oiled machine where everything is mechanical. The tone of ones voice would sound alike, we would probably look alike, live in the same perfect home with no color or music, because color and music induces emotions, and it is emotions that set us apart from machines.

The story of Jesus teaches us that even in death, after being brutally beaten and hanging from a cross for hours, we must forgive; including forgiving such extreme acts as crucifixion. Forgiveness no matter what!

Give – donate to a charity. Volunteer at a shelter, or a convalescent home, or be a big brother/big sister. Although there is no relationship between wealth and happiness, it is a known fact that happiness can be found through the act of giving. This sense of well-being is more than just feeling good about ourselves; giving connects us, if it is an act of compassion. Give compassion, receive compassion.

Just today I was thinking about buying some fresh cut flowers and passing them out at the hospital to visitors who look like they're in need of a sympathetic smile. You can almost always find someone in an I.C.U. (Intensive Care Unit) waiting room.

Make that heart to heart connection. It will make you high.

The fourth part of this recipe is **living in the now.** There's a book called, "The Power of Now," written by Eckhart Tolle that taught me something that I was quite unaware of. Happy people live in the moment.

In 2016, when Donald Trump won the presidential election, a friend called me first thing the following morning crying hysterically for fear of what a Trump leadership would do to our country. Her mind was flooded with thoughts of war, destruction, rampart racism, and every other dark speculation the imagination can conjure. And she wasn't the only one. The majority of the country was outraged and became very fearful.

In short, Eckhart Tolle writes, "Unease, anxiety, tension, stress and worry-all forms of fear—are caused by too much future, and not enough presence. Guilt, regret, resentment, grievances, sadness, bitterness, and all forms of non-forgiveness are caused by too much past and not enough presence."

> *"One of the happiest moments in life is when you find the courage to let go of what you can't change."*

If you're feeling dis-ease, stop and think about what your mind is harping on and then bring your thoughts to the hear and now. This moment in time is all that matters. You may not even be here tomorrow, so make the most of the moment at hand.

And of course, you can't have happiness without **love**. We love some more than others, but love is always there, and love is the award. Without love there is no meaning to life.

Hate is nothing more than a degree of love, a lack of love. And more often than not, when that person you think you hate leaves this planet, you feel nothing but love. All else disappears; the hate, the resentment, all gone!

My niece had a step-father, who really gave her a hard way to go when it comes to loving this man. One night when her son was spending the night with grandma, the boy awoke crying, in the wee morning hours, because he wasn't feeling well. So the step-dad calls my niece and says, "Come get your fucking kid. I don't want him to ever stay here again!"

My first reaction when I heard this story was one of shock and anger. I wanted belt the guy. I would never allow that dude to see my kid again, but at this point, its two weeks later, and the man has died, and my niece is seriously mourning him. She's posting his picture with her son on Facebook and referring to him as her son's grandfather.

Most of us would probably find it hard to relate to her sorrow, yet I have seen this happen many times. No doubt about it, love is a very natural human trait shared by all. Even the most hateful among us has some good tucked away inside somewhere. You just have to stand tall to see beyond the walls that hide the light.

It isn't the dark shadow that we hide, but the light. Being short and rude with people comes easy, but to truly stand naked and vulnerable with your heart on your sleeve is an act of bravery.

And don't forget to love yourself. Unhappy people will compare themselves to others. You don't want to be unhappy, know that you are unique. You were created to be just who you are, so that means God loves you. Love your craziness! Embrace it and shine on.

> *"Do what you feel in your heart to be right, for you'll be criticized anyway." – Eleanor Roosevelt*

Do not be so critical of yourself. Critical thinking focuses on the negative. If you are in the habit of criticizing yourself or others, Ron Potter-Efron, the author of, "Stop the Anger Now," suggests setting a goal for 24 hours to notice how many good things about yourself, the world and your surroundings as you can. Do this everyday for a month. This will assist in training your brain to think differently.

Second, Efron suggest that during those moments you when you see only the bad points of yourself, or a situation, that you set a goal to see the good. He further suggests using the following statement, "I could have complained about ___________, but instead I noticed ___________." The more we train ourselves to look for the good, the more we'll see it.

THE TEN COMMANDMENTS PLUS

Here's some old school advice to add flavor to your happiness. There are like these ten simple rules meant to secure happiness among the masses. They may be as old as Moses, but these simple instructions, if followed, can bring a lifetime of happiness.

First, "You should have no other God's before me." We are the children (extensions) of God, which means collectively we are God. No life is above or below another. Yet consumerism, capitalism, and corporate worship rule within our society. If we allow the almighty dollar (status) to carry more authority than the Almighty (love), then we're breaking rule number one right out the starting gate.

The second one is easy, "Don't use the Lord's name in vain." In other words, show some respect. War in the name of God could fall under this category as well, I believe; after all, another word for vain is narcissistic. God gave us these ten rules to keep the peace, not promote war and the killing that goes with it.

Third, take a day off and spend it outside among nature with your family and loved ones. Celebrate and praise the day. How can anyone not want to abide by this rule? This commandment gives us permission to be happy. So rejoice and be happy!

Fourthly, obey your elders regardless. If you do not respect your parents, then you do not respect yourself, for we are a stock of those who created us. You gotta love the bad, as well as the good, because all humans are made up of bad and good, including you. Like love, good just burns at different degrees at different times. So no matter how wrong you may feel about someone, respect their wisdom and their wishes.

Five – do not kill. There are no exceptions to this rule. Even Jesus upheld this one when Pilot's soldiers came to arrest him.

Peter drew his sword and struck the high priest's slave, cutting off his ear. Jesus scolded Peter and said, "Stop, no more of this!" Then he healed the man's ear. The story not only condemns the actions of His disciple, it serves as an example that any man who says he kills in the name of Jesus/God is full of himself. Jesus is so totally against this behavior that he added an eleventh commandment.

Six, keep your hands to yourself. Before marriage became a man-made contractual agreement between two people, it was a spiritual commitment first and foremost. When I married, it was on the beach in front of God and all to witness. Our wedding rings are engraved with three crosses upon them. Marriage is kind of like a promise to God too, because you can love someone in the name of God. You just can't kill in the name of God.

Seven, again, keep your hands to yourself. Do not steal. Be grateful. There's no need to steal. The Earth has much to share, and the universe loves to give.

Eight, be truthful; live with honor. There is no honor in being a liar. Although we do tend to lie to ourselves from time to time, the truth is never really hidden. Plugging your ears will not change it. A happy human will embrace the truth once realized.

Number nine and ten are in regards to jealousy and longing for what others have. Do not set your heart on someone or something that belongs to someone else, whether it be that person's spouse or property.

Then there's the eleventh commandment given by Jesus just before the crucifixion – love one another. In the end, Jesus taught us to forgive as well.

Love and gratitude are reiterated throughout the commandments given to us, yet as I look upon the people of Earth, I see a major lack of all the above.

As a collective, we have forgotten the simplicity of life. We've complicated living with governments within governments, and we live by hundreds of rules and laws that we've created all by ourselves. With each new law, we lose another freedom.

Still, no human is perfect and there will be times when each of us violates these commandments, and that's ok. But you have to be able to recognize and ask for forgiveness from time to time.

The sacrament of confession commonly practiced within the Catholic Church is a discipline that teaches one to recognize the sin within. And I believe it's this training of the mind is why I come in contact with more Catholic (or X-Catholics) truth seekers than any other religion.

> *"The more you know yourself, the less judgmental you become." - Aniekee Tochukwu Ezekiel*

There once was a group of four or five of us, who would meet once a week to discuss other beliefs and practice different forms of meditation, and I can only remember one of us who did not have heavy Catholic roots. And this group of people didn't meet in a church; we were from different points on the globe, and we weren't even of the same generation.

Personally, I have grown beyond a church, and I'm not advocating for one religion or another. I only wanted to point out a common denominator among those in search of a greater truth.

There's a gospel called Thomas that was once a part of the bible. Many believe the reason why the Church chose not to include it was because of this passage:

Jesus said, "I am the light that is over all things. I am all: from me all came forth, and to me all attained. Split a piece of wood; I am there. Lift a stone, and you will find me there." (Thomas 1:77)

A church is made of wood and stone. Clearly one does not need to go to church to be a Christian. To be a Christian you need only to practice the teachings of Christ. Live the way he taught us to live. That's all.

Keep life simple, don't make life so difficult and complicated that you make it difficult for others to love you. That is what I love the most about the last commandment. It is so simply stated – love one another. K.I.S.S. (Keep It Simple Stupid).

UNHAPPINESS

First off, there is no shame in being unhappy. No human being is ever happy all the time. There are all kinds of circumstances that can lead one to sadness. And being sad is not a bad thing. Actually, it's rather healthy to have a good cry now and then. Crying relieves stress and anxiety, which promotes mental health.

When I was a kid, my dad would poke fun at my mom when she would cry during a movie. I grew up thinking that crying was a weakness. I use to fight those tears like crazy when I watched a soulful film, because I was too worried about what others thought of me. Most times I had to walk out the room to keep from crying, or I would hide and wipe away my tears in private hoping no one seen me.

My dad on the other hand, whom I'm, sure, wanted to cry too, used humor to keep the tears at bay. He defended himself by poking fun at anyone who was about to drop a tear.

I eventually figured it out and now I release those emotions with a good cry. I let it out. I'd rather feel life then turn a stone cold shoulder to it, and I feel better for it.

Still, there are those little annoyances to avoid when it comes to achieving happiness. For some people it is easier to understand what not to do then to follow what to do. So if you wish to be happy, but find yourself doing any of the following, cease that behavior.

Take for instance the act of complaining. We all complain about our circumstances at one time or another. But when I hear myself complaining, I hear nothing but negativity running from my mouth as it flows into the ears of another, spreading like wild fire from one human to another.

Do not **complain**. To complain is to focus on the bad. Recognize the good in any given situation. The Universal Law of Polarity dictates that there are two sides to everything. Even the ego has a benefit as well as its drawbacks.

Do not try to **change others**. Accept people for who they are. Bottom line - if you want to change your world? Then focus on changing yourself. There's no way around it.

> *"The world as we have created it is a process of our thinking. It cannot be changed without changing our thinking." — Albert Einstein*

Do not **compare yourself to others**. This cannot be reiterated enough. It's such an easy trap to fall into. It will make you miserable. When you find yourself feeling jealous or unworthy, turn it around with some gratitude. Look at the good within your own life. It's there. You are gifted, and it's a unique presence to be shared with all of mankind. But if you're wasting energy by worrying about what others think of you, then your own uniqueness will never shine forth.

Do not **worry over future events**. It hasn't happened (yet)! It may not ever happen. Just remember to bring your thoughts to the present moment when you find yourself worrying over something that hasn't happened. Ask yourself, "In this present moment, what is it I need?"

Most times when I ask that question of myself, I have found that it' a beautiful sunny day and I only need to enjoy it. Puff! - Future thoughts gone. No more worry.

The same goes if you're dwelling on the past. If you find yourself feeling guilt or resentment; first, you need to forgive yourself, and/or that person who hurt you. And then you need to bring your thoughts to the present moment, because the present moment is the moment of truth. The person we were yesterday is not the person we are today. At least I hope not. Evolution is to grow; to learn from your mistakes and become a better person. This applies to those who have hurt us as well

Do not allow your **emotions to overwhelm you**. When we are young, our emotions run high. It's easy to get carried away and make a mole hill into a mountain. Find the courage to let go of what you cannot change. Overestimating the problem is underestimating yourself.

Do not **avoid your problems**. Avoidances will get you nowhere fast. The more you prolong an issue, the more it festers and occupies your thoughts and drains your energy.

Do not **attach yourself** to people, things, outcomes, statuses, etc. You are the captain of your ship. You might credit yourself as being a better person for knowing someone, but that someone does not make you who you are. The same goes for material items, like a hot red sports car. That car does not dictate who you are. If you play the stock market and lose your dead daddy's inheritance, it does not make you a loser. And status is nothing more than a false façade – you are human, period! No one is above you or below you.

Do not stay in **relationships that do not serve you**. Don't get me wrong, if you're married, then there are going to be those times when something comes along and shakes it all up. But if you are in a relationship where you are constantly being criticized, beaten upon, or you find yourself living with an energy sucking vampire, you may want to consider bailing.

Do not take everything so personally. **You cannot please everyone**. For every person who agrees with you, you can be sure there's another who does not. So if you're receiving some negative feedback, just remember that there is someone out there who supports you fully; most likely just as many people as those who oppose you.

Jesus said, "A person cannot mount two horses and bend two bows, and a slave cannot serve two masters, otherwise that slave will honor one and offend the other. - Thomas 1:47

Do not **play the victim**. And I am not only referring to the damsel in distress kind of victim, I'm talking about falling victim to an idea or belief. For example, you are involved in a car accident. Right away you have lawyers contacting you, and next you're seeing a doctor or a chiropractor, and they all tell you how badly you're feeling. Instead of your condition improving, you fall into that trap of helplessness, because they all have you believing you're disabled in some fashion or another. The body responds to the mind, meaning you can literally think yourself into sickness.

The same can be said for pharmaceutical commercials on television. If you hear something enough times, you can very well likely come to believe that you have or will have the disease that is associated with the pill of the day.

I remember when I saw the commercial for restless leg syndrome. I thought to myself, no way! Then one day I'm laughing about restless leg syndrome and my friend says she has that. Out of all the years that I had known this person, they had never told me they had restless leg syndrome, but hey, they do now. Now that someone gave it a name and told us that we need a pill to fix it.

To be a victim is to be powerless. The same can be said for **blaming others** for our troubles. We give up our power; we are no longer as strong and able as we once were, or could be. Our happiness decreases another degree or so.

You are the one behind the wheel. This is your life, your story, your responsibility. There is no co-author. No one can make life better or worse for you, only you have that power. Realize it and live it.

PART II – SPIRIT GUIDES

> *Jesus said the "Father's kingdom is spread out upon the earth, and people don't see it (Thomas 1:113).*

We are never alone. The trees, the wind, the rocks, the water, the animals, they all have spirit. Some of us seek advice through nature. Some of us look for guidance from angels and saints. Some of us pursue direction from the spirits of the dearly departed.

You may think you can fool your brothers and sisters here among the living, but in the spirit world eyes are upon you. What we do here on Earth is reflected within that world.

As an example, here is a vision that a dear friend of mine shared with me in regards to the spirit world. Her name is Melinda Shott. Melinda is a healer, and her vision came during Shavasana. For those not familiar with Shavasana, it is a Yoga pose where you lay flat on your back, arms at the side of your body and palms face up. It's a meditation that is usually conducted at the end of yoga exercises. The following is in her words.

"As I drifted in the peace of the dark rest with closed eyes, after having exerted & stretched body into openness, I found myself on a small rowing boat in the middle of the sea. As I moved out of the body to see the screen scene from the audience, I saw that the body was yours. "Oh! It's Kim" I said to myself. Then I went back into your body to experience whatever was being shown, because the feeling was sooooo attractive.

What happened next was nothing short of ecstasy. I was you, & we were in this rowing boat out in the middle of a most magnificent sea made of light filaments that permeated everything. It was a sea of light water & light sea animals that communicated to us (you) telepathically, & you were just soaking in the magnificence of be-ing. Ever so slowly you rowed the boat (even that was made of light) as you soaked in the communications from the ethers of the sea animals.

Then the most amazing thing happened! The sea animals began jumping into the air of light & swimming in it! It was a kaleidoscope of light infused sea animals all around, singing this symphony of sounds that took me (in your body) into even higher ecstasy. I stayed there until the yoga teachers voice brought me out of that state. And I found myself rowing the boat again ever so slowly in the ocean of light sea again.

So I asked, "What does this mean?" And I understood it is where you're traveling now, in the ethereal worlds, & that I'm to share this with you. The download showed that it's because in the material world you're feeling immense pain over the conditions of our seas. And that this pain doesn't need to be carried on your physical shoulders anymore. That you need to know about the work you are doing in other dimensions, simultaneously, because this time continuum is merely the illusion we create to evolve our consciousnesses, which are also collectively vibrating in spheres, as well."

At the time of Melinda's vision, I was somewhat conflicted between continuing as an environmental activist and a new direction that was unfolding before me, but I had not shared this information with Melinda. Yet, her message was timely, authentic, and most certainly appreciated.

Her vision also serves as an example of "Heaven on Earth." What we do here on Earth has in impact on the spirit world, as well as other possible dimensions. The spirits are always there to assist us; we just forgot how to communicate from an alternative level.

CHAPTER FIVE – COMMUNCATING WITH SPIRIT

We ask for help, but do we hear the answer when it is presented?

A man whispered, "God speak to me."

And a meadowlark sang. But the man did not hear.

So the man yelled, "God speak to me!"

And the thunder rolled across the sky. But the man did not listen.

Then the man looked around and said, "God, let me see you."

And a star shined brightly. But the man did not notice.

And the man shouted, "God, show me a miracle!"

And life was born. But the man did not know.

So then the man cried out in despair,

"Touch me God, and let me know you are here."

Whereupon God reached down and touched the man.

But the man brushed the butterfly away and walked on.

(Author Unknown)

First, I would like to say that we must make a request for guidance before spirit will work with us, because they cannot interfere with our free will. Spirit guides are not allowed to communicate with us, unless we allow it, by asking for their help. It is necessary to pose a question in order for there to be a communicated answer.

There are several ways in which spirit communicates with us.

It can be through nature, like the poem above suggest, or it can be in dreams, radio waves, and even through other people, like my friend Melinda sharing her vision with me, or a medium who speaks to the dead.

In 1998, I stumbled upon a book called, "Animal-Speak," by Ted Andrews. It totally turned my life around. It opened the door for me and taught me how to communicate with spirit through nature. It's like an ancient language of symbolism. Ted Andrews later came out with a book called, "Nature-Speak." I recommend it as well.

Take for instance the owl. Owls, by human standards, often represent wisdom. Some owls have orange or yellow eyes, and because most owls are nocturnal, it is said that the owl can shed light (yellow/orange eyes) on the darkness. In Christianity the owl is said to be symbolic of Jesus. But in some cultures the owl can have a negative attachment, such as death. It truly depends on your personal belief. What do you believe the owl to be?

You can search for suggestions in regards to symbolism of any animal, plant or tree but in the end, it's all up to your interpretation. Remember, heaven presides in the heart. What does your inner voice say to you?

When I see mourning doves, I see arch-angels, and I give them thanks for looking over us. That's me though. Not everyone sees the regal glory that I see and feel when I view these birds.

I consider hawks protectors. I see them often when I travel. Recently I took an eleven day road trip out west, and we saw a hawk daily on our travels, which removed any doubt of danger lurking along the road somewhere.

The crow traveled with us too. I call the crows the watchers. They are known to fly with wolves and warn of danger ahead, and on more than one occasion, they've kept me from getting a speeding ticket.

At our last stop before we returned home from our trip, I bought a coffee mug that has two horses facing each other, with a black bird in between the horses, as well as a black bird on the side of both horses. Horses represent travel and the crow had traveled the entire trip with us.

The cup serves as a beautiful symbolic gesture of our trip. The color black is symbolic of magic and creation, and our trip was indeed magical.

> *"If you talk to the animals, they will talk with you, and you will know each other. If you do not talk to them, you will not know them, and what you do not know you will fear. What one fears, one destroys." – Chief Dan George*

Once you learn the ways of the animals, life becomes so much more magical. There are some cultures that believe that when we are born the spirit of one animal volunteers to protect and guide us throughout our life. Maybe angels? Why not? For every pair of eyes there is someone looking through them.

Connect. Go outside and stand barefoot upon the soil of the earth. Simply being outdoors among nature has been proven beneficial for the health and well being of humans. Sit quietly with your palms tuned upward towards the sun with a quiet mind, and feel the sun's energy in the palm of your hands.

Open your ears and watch with your eyes. If spirit is looking to message you, you'll know it. Maybe it's a crow that keeps cawing out, or a frog that hops on you out of nowhere, something that makes you go "Wow" is most definitely a message.

Get on the Internet and type in "symbolic qualities of __________," and honor the messenger by learning what you can; maybe draw it or write about it; feel how it applies to your life.

Feed your creativity and keep a journal and learn at the same time. Incorporate your nature journal with a dream journal.

Dreams are another tool spirit uses to communicate with us. And by the way, communication works both ways.

If there is something weighing heavy on your mind, ask God or your angel a question. Matters of the heart will be addressed. Write your question out on a piece of paper before you go to bed at night. Tuck it under your pillow and keep your question in your mind as you fall asleep.

When morning comes, write about the dream right away, while it's fresh in the mind. Include colors, shapes, numbers, and how you feel during the dream and afterwards. All of these are clues as to the message of the dream.

There are free dream dictionaries available on the Internet to help you interpret the information. Again, only you can have the final say as to interpretation. And if you're keeping a journal, and you're unsure of yourself, you will eventually see a pattern and realize the message/answer to your question. You may even be dreaming of future events. One thing is for certain, you will never know if you do not take the time and keep a record of your dream adventures.

I have shared my dream journal with one person, and she loved it, so much so that she suggested I make book out of it just as it is. Dreams are cool and they can spark creativity effortlessly all on their own for sure.

When you make a heartfelt effort to connect and learn, spirit is more than willing to oblige. And the more you track your dreams and nature encounters, the deeper your belief will become.

And it is not uncommon to mindfully ask a question and receive an answer immediately, especially if you are in the moment and your mind is clear. You'll know when this happens, because it's a wow thing, like "Wow that was fast!"

Cloud reading is another way of communicating with spirit. You can get a quick response, but of course it helps if it's a windy cloudy day. Close your eyes and meditate on your question, remember to ask from the heart; do this for five minutes or so, then open your eyes and describe the image(s) you see in the cloud(s). What does that image symbolize to you? How does it relate to your question?

Spirit can be found on the **radio waves** too. One time I was being followed by a private investigator, but I didn't know it. Not until a song came on the radio called, "Somebody's Watching Me."

I was involved in a law suit at the time, so it didn't surprise me when I pulled up into a grocery store parking lot and watched for a tail. Sure enough, I had seen this woman in a restaurant earlier in the day on the other side of town. So I approached her car. When she seen me coming, she did a three-sixty head turn in other direction and refused to look my way. Yeah, she was following me alright. A friend ran the tag for me, and it turned out that she was a P.I. from the next town over.

You are never alone. Spirit is always there to guide and protect us. You simply have to be aware of what is happening around you. Be conscious of your thoughts.

CHAPTER SIX – THE BOOK OF DREAMS & OTHER THINGS

"Why, then, do you make complaint against him that he gives no account of his doings? For God does speak, perhaps once, or even twice, though one perceive it not. In a dream, in a vision of the night, (when deep sleep falls upon men) as they slumber in their beds." Job 33:13-15

The bible demonstrates from the very beginning that dreams are symbolic messages from God. Genesis chapter forty is literally about dream interpretation. At Genesis 40:5, *"the cupbearer and the baker of the king of Egypt who were contained in the jail both had dreams on the same night, each with its own meaning."*

It was Joseph who interpreted the dreams and commissioned God as the conveyer. Joseph asked the cupbearer to share his dreams with him.

The cupbearer says, *"In my dream, I saw a vine in front of me, and on the vine were three branches. It had barely budded when its blossoms came out, and in its clusters ripened into grapes. Pharaoh's cup was in my hand; so I took the grapes, pressed them out into his cup, and put it in Pharaoh's hand,"* Genesis 40:9-11.

Joseph then shares his interpretation, *"This is what it means, the three branches are three days; within three days Pharaoh will lift your head and restore you to your post. You will be handling Pharaoh his cup as you formerly used to do when you were his cupbearer."*

The baker was so impressed that he asked Joseph to interpret his dream as well. So the baker says, *"I had three wicker baskets on my head; in the top one were all kinds of bakery products for Pharaoh, but the birds were pecking at them out of the basket on my head,"* Genesis 40:16-17.

Joseph tells the baker, *"The three baskets are three days; within three days Pharaoh will lift your head and have you impaled on a stake, and the birds will be pecking flesh from your body,"* Genesis 40:18-19.

Not only do these dreams come to light just as Joseph had predicted, but in the very next chapter, Joseph interprets the Pharaoh's dream as well.

The Pharaoh's dream goes like this, *"He saw himself standing by the Nile, when out of the Nile came seven cows, handsome and fat; they grazed in the reed grass. Behind them seven other cows, ugly and gaunt, came up out of the Nile; and standing on the bank of the Nile beside the others, the ugly, gaunt cows ate up the seven handsome fat cows,"* (Genesis 41:1-4).

The Pharaoh awakes, and then falls back to sleep has a second dream. *"He saw seven ears of grain, fat and healthy growing on a single stock. Behind them sprouted seven ears of grain, thin and blasted by the east wind; and the seven thin ears swallowed up the seven fat, healthy ears."*

Genesis 41:25, *"God has thus foretold Pharaoh what he's about to do."* In the end, Joseph saves Egypt from a seven-year drought, by stockpiling seven good years of food, in preparation of seven years of drought and hunger.

There are more than thirty entries in the bible that refer to dreaming or dreams. Four of those occasions can be found in the New Testament.

> *"Should there be a prophet among you, in visions I will reveal myself to him, in dreams I will speak to him." – Numbers 12:6*

The cupbearer and the baker were not prophets or kings. God speaks to all of us. You simply have to believe. That's all.

From this point on, I will share a few of my own dreams and visions with you. And as these dreams will demonstrate, a journal can be somewhat amusing, as well as insightful.

DREAM: THE MUSIC BOX *(Jun 7, 1999) – I'm in what resembles a box car. The train is standing still. I wonder why the train isn't moving. There are other people with me. I then look back into the car I'm on, and a small curly blond hair girl is sitting on a bed, and my dog Katie is laying there as well. I look back out the door and a music box is handed to me, but I don't know from who it is.*

The gift is pretty. It's like a small ceramic merry-go-round with horses. I love it.

It is now October 10, 2007, and I find myself taking a Creative Visualization Class. All of my classmates and my instructor are strangers to me. It's the last class before Thanksgiving. We've been instructed to bring in a gift. It must be something we cherish, but are ready to release, so that we make room for the new. This concept of non-attachment is practiced in Hinduism and Buddhism. So this is my story as to what happened.

Larry gave Jenny a horse (ass trophy), and I received a round music box from a blonde curly girl. And directly in front of the building where this class is taking place sits a train that stands still; it never moves, there are no train tracks. And this same story continues with another dream I had.

DREAM: KING SOLOMON *(Feb 15, 2005) – I'm in a wooden house. There are people coming and going. There's a conveyor belt type thing in the middle of the room. It brings water up into the house.*

Next, I'm in the front yard of a house of stone, and I want to get to the backyard. Some guy see's me and tells me, if I like, I can cut though the house to get to the backyard. I walk into a large stone room. It's beautiful. There are large windows facing the backyard that are as long as the ceiling to the floor, with pillars in front of them. I notice water from the ocean splashing along the bottom of the windows. I wonder why the water does not leak into the house.

I walk to the windows and look out in awe. There's a giant conveyor belt type deal that brings water up to the house; this is why the water splashes along the bottom of the windows. There are children playing and climbing along the rafters that bring the water up to the house.

Right before I wake up, the name King Solomon is said.

I had this dream before the October 10th Creative Visualization Class. The gift that I brought to that last class, before Thanksgiving, was a cross that I made in honor of the dream that I just described. Because there was an odd amount of students in the class, my gift went to our class instructor; her birthday is February 15th, the same date as the morning of the dream. She too had curly blonde hair.

I would like to note that I had no clue what-so-ever as to who would receive my gift before the class. Names were drawn the day of, when we arrived.

Considering that she was a spiritual teacher and that the dream was of King Solomon, who is known for his wisdom, the gift was certainly appropriate. And the dream itself symbolized a new beginning for me spiritually. The Creative Visualization class was the first of many metaphysical classes that I participated in that had a positive impact on my life.

DREAM: THE CORNERSTONE *(Aug 24, 2005) – An old woman tells me she had a dream about me. She's smiling. All I can see is her red lips. The red freaks me out. I'm afraid she's going to* *tell me when I'm going to die. So I wake up.*

When I fell asleep again, I'm told to put down three rocks, and to stand on the other side of them for protection. There's one rock already there. I wonder how I am to lay the rocks down.

There is now a set of feet in from of me. They are Jesus' feet. He tells me how to sit the rocks onto the ground. Jesus is on the other side of the rocks, where I am to stand. I lay the rocks out right to left, with the third rock sitting slightly in front of the existing fourth rock.

In this dream, the old woman is a symbol of wisdom. The red freaks me out because red is often symbolic of warning. But it is also a symbol of love and passion.

The number three, for me personally, is the number of spirituality; the Father, Son, and the Holy Spirit. There is already one rock lying on the ground at the side of Jesus' feet. This rock I'm sure is the foundation of His ministry. Rocks symbolize strength, integrity, and commitment as well as foundations.

I am very passionate and committed to living as the Creator intended us to live. I asked the Creator for the Wisdom of Solomon, and in the past nineteen years that is what I have been handed.

This book you are reading is the second book I've written in regards to spirituality. Maybe the books are the rocks, and there will be a third. Because I learn something new every day; wisdom is never ending.

***CLOUD READING*:** Hair flows from the crown chakra and symbolizes higher spiritual power; the longer the hair the more the power. The dog is playful. There are two tails, the dogs and the pony tail in hand. The past is behind you (tail end). The word that resonates here is "Transition."

DREAM: THE DANCING BEAR *(Oct 16, 2014) – We're standing on the beach. To my left in the distance I see a bear chasing a bird in front of the stores/restaurants. Eventually he finds his way to the other side of the wall that divides the stores from the beach. On his hind legs he chases the flying bird in the air. The bird is white, maybe a sea gull. I thought he looked pretty cute* *chasing the bird.*

I point this out to someone who is sitting on my left. They're all up about it.

I turn to walk away, when someone says, "Don't be scared," just as I turn back looking over my shoulder. The bear is running in our direction along the wall. I don't know if the bear is friendly or not, and I do not trust it.

The bear is often associated with healing medicine. A sea gull symbolizes responsible behavior. A standing bear is symbolic of a need to defend your beliefs, and if the bear is chasing you, it could possibly mean you are avoiding an issue in your life. Animals in general are often associated with the second and third chakras (the digestive system). In addition, restaurants and beaches are places of nourishment.

And it wasn't only in a dream I saw the bear. It kept popping up on television and in Facebook post. At the time of the dream, I thought I possibly had a bladder infection and was treating myself with herbal remedies, in the form of a blood purification, which meant a change in my diet as well. But apparently I was wrong in my interpretation of the dream.

Although the blood purification seemed to have solved the problem, two months later (December 16th) to the date of the dream, I found myself in the emergency room. My large intestines had ruptured and poison had spread throughout my body. It wasn't a bladder infection that I was fighting, it was diverticulitis; an inflammation of the bowels and colon.

Drumming
July 16, 2015

DRUMMING VISION: *When I was drumming this afternoon, a vivid image of a naked Buddha came to my mind. He had butterfly wings, and he was happy to be drumming.*

Nudity = acceptance. Buddha is symbolic of wisdom and inner spirituality. And butterflies are symbolic of joy and spirituality, and suggest possibly a new way of thinking.

At the time of the vision, I was reading The Power of Now, by Eckhart Tolle (a new way of thinking). The book says when you are living in the now, everything will seem to glow. I stepped outside and everything looked so vibrant. Kind of like the naked Buddha with butterfly wings. The dirt under the tree was reddish brown and everything seemed to have a glow to it, like it had rained, but it wasn't wet.

DREAM: THE ROBBERY *(2002) – I'm returning from a pizza delivery. I pull up to the back of the pizza shop. We're being robbed. There are three men lined up from the back door to the parking lot. The first man is white, and he has a knife; the second man is different. I don't know how, but he's different. The third man is black, and he has a gun. They are face to face with store managers.*

I was working part-time evenings for Donato's Pizza, in Columbus, Ohio, as a delivery driver, when this dream came to me. That evening as I pulled into the plaza parking lot, after a delivery, a black man with a gun ran out the front door towards the back parking lot.

It wasn't until later when I shared the dream with one of the managers that I found out that the black man was the third person to rob that particular store; three robbers "different" times, different managers.

If I didn't keep a journal, I would have missed out on the magic this life has to offer. Dreams like the Robbery reinforced my belief and my fascination with my nighttime visions. The Robbery was a dream that came to flourish immediately.

Whereas, dreams such as the Music Box and King Solomon came to be years later. Even the Dancing Bear dream was two months in the future, and if I would have interpreted it correctly, and went to a doctor to get checked out, I might have been able to avoid that life threatening event all together. But now I see. And the next time I dream of a bear, I will have a better understanding of how it applies to my life.

Another perspective on the bear dream is that in the dream I was told not to be fearful. Maybe that was the message? Like no matter what, I had to go through this life event in order to have a deeper understanding of myself and my purpose upon this planet, "but don't be scared; it'll be ok."

And you know what, I wasn't scared. I was prepared to die. Fear didn't creep into my bones until I came home and realized I was going to live and deal with the harsh reality of some substantial physical changes to my body. It wasn't dying that I feared, but living.

> *"The world is so big, and we're so small. Sometimes it feels like you can't do anything at all. But the world can be better, in spite of its flaws. The world can be better, and you'll be the cause. And even though the waves are bigger than our boat, the wind keeps us sailing, as love gives us hope. Some days it's darker, but we'll keep rowing, because people like you whisper, ;Keep going, keep going, keep going.'" – Kid President (Soul Pancake)*

We humans are powerful, much more powerful than we realize. Each of us has a gift to share. Realize who you are and live up to your potential. You might not like what you dream or what you see, but remember, every day is a new day, and change is a human right. If you do not like what you see in your dreams, then change your reality. Spirit is here to guide us and assist us, not hurt us. Only we can do that. The choice is always ours to make.

CHAPTER SEVEN – HONOR & CEREMONY

Spirit guides, angels and saints should always be honored in some fashion. Even if it's a simple thank you. Always thank your spirit guides.

What we do here on Earth reflects in the spirit world. Sometimes I will honor mine by sharing a story, or posting a photo on the internet. Earlier in this book, I shared one story where I laid out white shells on the beach to honor an angel who had been watching over me.

I sometimes will create three wooden crosses during Lent, and then give them away on Easter, or place them in the sand dunes along the beach. I would work on the crosses daily, by burning images into stories onto the wood, and then I would paint them and add bird feathers that came to me in the past year. It was a daily Lenten ceremony. It was my way of honoring Jesus, whom I consider to be a spirit guide and teacher.

If it is an animal that assists you, you could possibly make a donation to a charity that represents that particular creature. The wolf for instance comes to you in a dream; you could make a monetary donation to save the wolves. Or sign a petition to protect wolves. If you like to draw, or you are an artist of sorts, you can apply your craft and create a wolf. Whatever you choose to do know that killing an animal is not a way of honoring it.

In the year 2010, when BP's Deepwater Horizon spewed oil all over the Gulf of Mexico, there were a lot of sad people. I never thought I would see the day that oil would wash up on our beaches. It was a very dark time indeed. Then the sadness turned to anger, and blame and everyone forgot to love the water, because they were too busy shouting about how tainted and toxic it was.

Thank God I had a friend who turned my head around by starting a little group who got to together once a month to honor the water and help the Gulf of Mexico heal.

We would go to the beach and collect small jars of water, and take the water home and meditate on it. I took words like love, gratitude, and healing and taped them to the jar, and I would draw a smiley face on the jar somewhere. Then we would gather again on or near the full moon and share stories, poems, or just thoughts in regards to the water. Then as a group we would meditate and then release the water back into the Gulf of Mexico, with the intention that the water would heal all that it touches.

That is a ceremony; a way of honoring the water. And you do not need a group of people to perform such a custom. You can do the very same thing all on your own.

Keep the ceremony simple. It does not have to be an extravagant event. Spirit is more impressed with what lies within our heart than size of our ego. Always pray from the heart.

Prayer sticks can add power to your prayers. A prayer stick is just as it sounds. You begin with a stick from a tree. Different trees have different energies. Oak is a hard wood; it symbolizes strength and endurance. Pine trees can reveal secretes. Palm on the other hand can represent happy returns and protection. You can use the internet to discover the symbolism of your tree/stick.

You can paint or use markers, or use a wood burning tool and add symbols to the stick. If it's a healing prayer stick, you might want to burn the archangel Raphael's name onto the stick; he is known as the healing angel, as mentioned in the bible, in the Book of Tobit.

Or draw an owl for wisdom; but never use owl feathers in a healing ceremony in which the feathers touch the person who is being helped. It is said that owl feathers can draw the sickness deeper into the body.

You may want to use a chakra color that correlates with the

area that is in need of healing, and paint the color onto the stick somewhere; a simple slash will work.

Next you want to tie a feather to the stick. The feather activates the prayer. Just like trees, different birds have different energies. Again, the book, "Animal-Speak," by Ted Andrews is an excellent reference to learning about animal symbolism. As a matter of fact, it was his book that taught me about prayer sticks.

One day my sister was in a lot of pain, so much so that she went to the hospital. The pain medication they were giving her was not working. My mother was so concerned that she called me crying.

So I journeyed to the middle world, and asked to be shown the affected area. I was shown a body with a glow from the chest down to the groin area. The glow was like a triangle hovering over the body. Then I was shown a snake (the serpent symbolizes the spine).

I asked, how can this be fixed? I was shown a parrot. The parrot was red, orange and blue (Parrots symbolize color healing). Red energizes the base chakra and strengthens energy. Blue is good for inflammation; orange is good for the muscular system.

So I made a prayer stick right away. I have big live oak trees (strength) throughout my yard, so it was no problem to find a stick lying on the ground. I stripped away the bark and sanded the stick down. It was about thirteen inches long.

I burned my sister's name onto the stick, with a parrot and a snake climbing up the stick. I also burned the symbol of Raphael (the healing angel) with a cross and the sun.

I painted the parrot the way I had envisioned it. Then I tied parrot feathers with the colors I was shown in the vision. I have a friend who had worked in a pet store that had given me many parrot feathers over the years. So I had everything I needed.

I then took the stick and placed in the sacred place under a tree in my yard. I said my prayer and then I left the stick in the ground for three days. I called my sister on the third day, and she was home and feeling much better.

It turned out that fibromyalgia was the cause of her dis-ease. Fibromyalgia is a muscular condition (orange). It most certainly can show up in the body as inflammation (blue), although the pain is believed to be a result of the central nervous system (red).

Fibromyalgia does not lead to death or muscle damage, and I'm sure the hospital did a fine job relieving her pain, once they knew what they were dealing with.

Still, simply meditating on the colors as I painted the stick and tied the feather to it is a healing gesture. Thoughts are powerful, and when you focus your attention like that, you give your prayers a powerful boost.

As part of my morning ritual, when I awake, I light a candle and incense, or I burn some sage, and I pray the rosary. Some say prayers are not a form of meditation, but if you focus on a particular thought while you pray, then it is meditative, just as chanting is considered a form of meditation.

When I shower, sometimes I'll do seven ohms as a way to center myself before thanking the water and shutting it off.

If I see a clock, and three or four numbers that are the same, like 3:33 or 11:11, I say a prayer, and if I can't say it immediately because I'm having a conversation, I'll say it to myself when I do get a chance.

If a bad storm approaches, I'll burn blessed palm, from Palm Sunday and ask the Holy Mother to protect us. Native American's refer to the Earth as Mother. I believe they are one in the same.

Just as we honor spirit, we should honor the Earth. Pick a day and gather trash on the beach, or sign a petition to stop the exploration of oil and gas in the ocean, or take part in a protest. Defend the Earth as you would your mother, after all it's a creation of God. Disrespect the Earth and in turn you are disrespecting the Creator.

And for those who say praying to Mary is blaspheme, Mary is like that friend who has a son who can help you out of a jam. Praying to Mary, the Mother of Jesus is no different than asking a saint or an angel for assistance.

If someone is sick, I pray to the archangel Raphael for a healing. If I see someone driving recklessly, I ask St. Christopher to protect that person and all those who come across their path. If I see a dog running lose near the road, I'll ask St. Francis to protect that animal.

And furthermore, throughout the New Testament the emphasis is on Mary as well as Jesus. The reason why I believe there is no mention of Joseph, after the virgin birth is because the story isn't a family story, but rather a story honoring the feminine and the masculine aspects of spirituality.

Mary/Woman = Birth Jesus/Man = Death

All four of the gospels begin with the birth of Jesus, and/or John the Baptist (water = birth). Mary is just as much, or even more so, the focus in the story of the birth of Jesus. She's a virgin for Christ sakes!

Look at the symbolism. Right before a woman gives birth, her water breaks; we are surrounded by water when we are in our mother's womb.

> *"What massacre happens to my son between him living within my skin, drinking my cells, my water, my organs, and his soft psyche turning cruel? Does he not remember he is half woman?" - Nayyirah Waheed (American poet)*

All four gospels end with death and rebirth. And the greatest story of Jesus is the death and resurrection. Death and birth are one in the same. Like the seasons, the tree may lose its leaves in the winter and appears dead, but come the spring time, it is born once again.

I would have to say at the very least that you cannot honor one without the other (birth/feminine and death/masculine), for they are one in the same, as is with mother and child.

> *"Then he said to his disciple, 'Behold, your mother.'" - John 19:27*

The definition of the word disciple is a follower, as in, "Follower, behold your mother."

Mary is the spirit mother of the followers of Jesus. It's kind of like how the Native American's refer to the Earth as Mother. Mary is often depicted in blue and white, the colors of the water and clouds. Earth and water are the feminine elements of life, whereas fire and air are considered masculine.

Take for instance the sun (fire) in the sky; it is symbolic of the Son of God; the light of God, who is often referred to in the masculine sense. And the wind, it moves and shapes as it stirs things up, just like Jesus did.

Feminine = Goodness   Masculine = Strength

There is a balance to be achieved in this life. It's like Ying and Yang. Ying is the blackness that absorbs color; the feminine – Yang is the whiteness that reflects color; the masculine. Together they complete the circle, slightly spiraled and balanced.

Within the human body, the left side of the body is generally considered the receptive side (feminine), and the right side of the body, the assertive side (masculine). But when it comes to the human brain, the sides switch. The left brain is considered to be a masculine energy, and right brain thinkers are feminine in nature.

We all have ying and yang within us. The lesson is to balance the feminine within as well as the masculine. In a world completely out of balance, out-weighed in masculinity, I find it somewhat refreshing to sit in the presence of such a blessed feminine energy as I pray the rosary.

Ritualistic acts are a demonstration of the dedication one holds in a belief. It's like you might not be able to hug God directly or kiss Spirit, but you can do little things to show your gratitude and appreciation. And as the saying(s) goes, it's the little things that count, and actions speak louder than words.

Honor and celebrate those in the spirit world. They love to be recognized, and rightfully so.

PART III – THE HOLISTIC FIX

The word holistic refers to the whole. Not only should the physical ailment be addressed but the mental and spiritual as well. The spirit has power over the mind, and the mind has power over the body. They are interconnected.

Say for instance, diverticulitis. On a metaphysical level, it is said that diverticulitis is a disease caused by blaming others and refusing to forgive them.

Diverticulitis damn near killed me. It is a very painful inflammation and infection of the intestines. I didn't even know I had diverticulitis until my intestines ruptured, and I found myself in the hospital for 17 days. I spent quite a bit of time within the hospitals critical care unit.

A friend of mine told me of the metaphysical aspects of diverticulitis, and my first thought was of my mom. But I thought I had forgiven her, so I shook it off.

Then five months later that I found myself in the hospital with the exact same problem, a puncture in the pipeline so to speak. The doctors determined that I was too weak for surgery, and sent me home after two weeks in the hospital, with drain tubes extending from my sides. Three little plastic containers that they referred to as grenades captured and contained the poison from inside my body.

The very same day I was released, my mom was admitted in a hospital up North, in Ohio, after suffering from a stroke. When that happened, I knew I had to dig deeper and do some forgiving. Something wasn't right. My world was falling apart. I come from a very strong willed healthy family, where this kind of thing just doesn't happen. Never in a million years did I dream that I'd find myself in this condition, and now my mom.

And at that moment I closed my eyes and saw myself taking my power back as my fist cracked the ground beneath. "I am strong," I told myself, "This shall cease now!"

I then visualized my mom and I connected to the source above with a stream of white light. The power that flowed through me I shared with my mom here on Earth, forming a triangle of light beaming directly from me to her. I held this thought for quite a while. Afterwards I felt so energized, I could hardly sleep.

Two or three days later, my mom was discharged from the hospital. No side effects, even though there was evidence that she had suffered minor strokes in the past. That was two years ago, and we're both doing fine today.

I may have forgiven my mom years ago in my mind, but apparently on a higher/spiritual level there was more work to be done. I love my mother dearly and feel closer to her than ever before. Another defensive wall fell away from around my heart.

And that is what holistic healing is all about. We have to examine our thoughts and heal our spirit when we find ourselves in physical distress. Otherwise we may never completely heal from the dis-ease.

Take diabetes. On a metaphysical level, diabetes is believed to be an indicator of emotional desolation on a spiritual level; someone who is unable to obtain the sweetness or the nectar of life. I've been there.

Life is to be savored! It is supposed to be sweet. Find the good in all situations and focus on it, instead of the bad. I became a much happier person when I switched it up.

The first two parts of this book were dedicated to healing the mind and the spirit, but the story wouldn't be complete if the physical aspects of healing were not addressed as well.

CHAPTER EIGHT – HEALER, HEAL THYSELF

Do you believe everything that is said on television? Is T.V. truth? Is the bible truth? Both are often used to manipulate the masses. Both were created by humans. You know us flawed creatures, we tend to put a personal slant on everything we do and say. There's no getting around that free will thing referred to as the ego.

Take doctors for instance, they are human. There's only so much time in a day and yet we rely on them for their knowledge to heal, while taking no responsibility of our own. Oh yeah, we might take the medications in the manner prescribed, but our liability should never end there.

Do some research, and investigate the drugs you were prescribed. Medical professionals are approached by pharmaceutical companies daily. These drug pushers are no different than those who stand on a street corner actively slinging their own brand of illegal comfort. There's a saying gaining popularity among the masses, "The pharmaceutical industry does not create cures, they create customers."

According to a May 2017, AARP Bulletin article, the pharmaceutical industry spent $24 billion dollars in 2016 marketing to health care professionals. Global Data, an analysis research company, revealed that 9 out of 10 pharmaceutical companies spend more on marketing than on research. A whopping $6.4 billion is spent in advertising to the American people annually. They are literally pushing drugs in your face right there in your living room.

Not only are there American's requesting these new drugs that were pushed through the FDA (Federal Drug Administration), as if there is a race as to who can get there first, but we are also likely making ourselves sick at the same time. If the mind is objected to repetitive thoughts, such as television commercials, the body can most certainly mimic the dis-ease. It's a proven fact.

AARP reported that drug companies spent $19.8 million dollars on politicians in 2016, and then was credited with $1.76 billion in orphaned drug tax credits. The same article goes on to say that CEO's of pharmaceutical companies make more money than any than any other industry, with an average annual salary of $14.5 billion. Talk about egotistical!

There's another saying gaining popularity, "The Earth provides for all our needs." I'm not a medical professional, but personal experience has taught me that type 2 diabetes and high cholesterol can be controlled by diet and herbs.

When my doctor first put me on a statin for cholesterol, I got on the Internet and did some research regarding statins. I read that statins kill good cholesterol as well as the bad. And in February 2012, the FDA informed health providers that statins are linked to an increased risk of type 2 diabetes. To further this statement, a Medscape article published in March 2015, reported a 46% increase in diabetes for those who had taken a statin for 6 years. The higher the dose and the longer the statin was taken the higher the risk.

So I stopped taking the drug, limited my consumption of red meat, fried foods, cheese, cream, and beer, and found a supplement that aids in building good cholesterol that also lowers the bad cholesterol at the same time. I also added more fruits to my diet.

And when my doctor told me I had pre-diabetes, a month later, I got on the Internet again and did some more research. I have never been a big soda drinker, but I do enjoy a little chocolate snack in the evening from time to time, and I still do.

In my research, I discovered that Jerusalem Artichokes, a vegetable, can decrease or eliminate the use of insulin. Other herbal remedies include Siberian Ginseng, which reduces blood sugar as well as cholesterol. Uva Ursi leaves are good for combating diabetes too. Burdock Root provides an abundance of iron and insulin. Cilantro leaves and stems can lower blood sugar. And Cinnamon (high grade) is a spice that lowers blood sugar as well as blood pressure, and bad cholesterol, while raising good cholesterol.

A lot of what I've mentioned can be purchased as a food, tea or a tincture at a health food store. The Jerusalem Artichokes I ordered online at Amazon.com.

So I incorporated these foods and herbs in my diet, while discontinuing beer, and potatoes, because carbohydrates are said to be the biggest enemy in sugar diabetes, more so than chocolate. And I brought my numbers down.

Diverticulitis on the other hand, became common in the United States in the 1990's, with a 50% increase since the year 2000, according to the Mayo Clinic in Rochester, Minnesota. No one knows the cause of diverticulitis, but according to Harvard Health Publications, one-third of Americans over the age of 60 will develop it.

As victim of diverticulitis, I have to ask, what are we putting in our bodies?

There is a man named Joseph Marx who wrote a book called, "Victory Over Cancer!" Joseph had a very aggressive esophageal cancer and was given only a 17% chance to live. In an interview with WEAR ABC, in February 2017, he said he rid himself of the tumor by simply changing his diet.

His cancer later returned though. So, Joseph did some more digging and found that methionine, and amino acid found mainly in meats, fish and dairy products, is like food to cancer. If you restrict it from your diet, you starve the cancer. At the time of the interview, after chemo, radiation and surgery, his cancer had been in remission for 9 months.

It's also suggested that high potassium foods can prevent cancer. "Cancer cells cannot live in a high potassium environment," according to Humbart Santillo, BS, MH, in his book, "Natural Healing With Herbs – The First American System of Herbology."

High potassium foods include: horseradish, onions, garlic, bananas, asparagus, cantaloupe, broccoli, lemon, grapes, grapefruit, dandelion greens, oranges, peaches, pears, plumes watermelon, raisins, oats, and pineapple, just to name a few.

Just beware that too much potassium can be dangerous as well. Avoid potassium supplements. Diet or protein drinks and diet bars often contain this mineral as well. Certain birth control pills and non-steroidal anti-inflammatory drugs can affect potassium levels too. If your potassium levels are too high, you may experience weakness, numbness, and/or tingling.

Ask questions and seek alternatives. I wouldn't be here today if it wasn't for the doctors and nurses who helped me on my way, but we cannot depend on them for our complete wholeness and health. There just isn't enough time in a day for them to keep up with all the new information after treating patients all day.

Do the research. If you don't have a computer, go to a public library. Most libraries have computers and most librarians are willing to help you. If you are researching an herb, always add the word "risk" with "benefits" of that particular food or herb. And always confer with your doctor.

Knowledge is a powerful tool, so don't be afraid to feed your mind, and believe in yourself. You know your own self better than anyone on this Earth plain. Not everyone's body is the same either. Still, I know that there inside your mind, beyond your ego, is a spiritual being capable of great feats; I know, because I've been there.

Some things cannot be seen by the eyes. When I was first admitted into the hospital after back to back surgeries, a battle raged within me that the doctors and nurses had no power to fix or even influence, regardless of the amount of pain numbing medication.

At one point, a black bird flew from my chest, and then some symbols came from within me and circled the bird, but it was the Eye of Ra that stood before me at five after on a clock; the third eye. The things I was seeing and feeling at that time are hard to explain, but I remember the feeling of fleeting fear as the bird bolted from within me, and it was cold. When I think back to that moment today, I still feel that fear; the fear to live.

It is said that the third eye is a call to accept this world as ours and to heal and love it. So I find myself writing this book with hope to heal the world I have created.

Major life events such as near death experiences have historically been viewed as life changing happenings. But what most people do not understand is that this new found change is not simply a result of nearly losing life, but a consequence of one who chooses life, when confronted with death.

It really is up to us as to whether we want to live or not. Only when we hand that responsibility over to others do we relinquish our power; our strength; our ability to heal. Like everything else in this existence, it's a use it or lose it scenario.

CHAPTER NINE – DEATH

A priest once told me that life is all about preparing for death. Life has taught me his words are true. We really should be living as if today is our last day on Earth.

All four of the Gospels begin with the baptism and birth of Jesus, and they all end with the death of Jesus. The story in between is one of great deeds and the brotherhood of man. Jesus lived his life as an example so we may learn. His greatest legacy was the resurrection; overcoming death.

I know of a man who wanted to be buried beside his grandmother, when his time comes, because he considers her to be a saint. He thought is that if he is to be buried beside her then he might have chance of going to heaven (verses hell I guess).

He knows in his heart that he has not lived as his grandmother would have wanted him to live.

Since it is impossible for him to be buried beside her, he now goes to church every Sunday with the hope of salvation for his soul.

I'm not saying that there's a hell, but what I am saying is don't wait till it's too late to be a fruitful human being. Wouldn't it be far more intelligent to live your life as if there is a God (or a place called hell), then to live as if there is no God and then die and find out your wrong?

A young man in his twenties died of cancer in my home, before I it became my home. His family had placed a hospital bed in the living room, by the large windows that faces out to the front of the house, and that is where he died.

Soon after we moved into our new Florida home, the neighbor from across the street knocked at our door. She practically fell into the house when I greeted her. It was clear that she was in somewhat of a panic.

Now, I had felt this kid's presence in the home on several occasions when sitting in the living room. So I asked the neighbor from across the street if she had seen someone other than my wife or I in the window.

Without hesitation she nodded yes. She then proceeded to tell us the story about this young man who had passed away in our house. His name was Carlos.

Later when no one was around I asked Carlos why he was still here. A strong sense came over me that he was afraid to move on because he was afraid he was going to go to hell.

So I talked to Carlos, and told him it was ok and that the light can do no harm. Then I urged him to follow that light. Later I smudged the house, and I haven't felt Carlos since then.

> *"The fear of death follows from the fear of life. A man who lives fully is prepared to die at any time." –*
> *Mark Twain*

When you are prepared to die there is no fear of death, because you are prepared. And it takes a lifetime of preparation that involves far more than attending a church once a week. Every day is a new challenge; a new lesson; a new opportunity to become a better human being than you were yesterday.

Don't fall into that trap that you are a good person just the way you are and no improvement is necessary. Life is like a balancing act. You're walking a wire and all of these outside influences and changes are flying about you, challenging your ability to keep the balance; to keep your focus on the here and now.

When I was a kid and my parents divorced they switched us kids from a Catholic School to a public schools – all endings (death) have a new beginning (birth). Some of us go to college after high school, and then marriage, and maybe children and/or divorce. You have been dying and reinventing yourself all your life.

Don't be afraid to live. Experience the people and the love, joy, and the sadness and suffering. Live. Feel it all, but without the fear.

Quite a few of us out there are fearful of death. Fear and death seem to go hand in hand; fear of the unknown I guess. If you find yourself afraid of mice, it is because you've never sat down to get to know a mouse. The same can be said about the Creator. If you truly have a relationship with God then there is no reason to be fearful of anything. If you say you *believe* in Jesus, which is the resurrection of life, then how can you fear death?

True freedom is living a life without fear. That is the legacy of Jesus. Live like death is nothing more than another stage in life, like college and marriage; another end with another beginning. No regrets!

Yes, we all make mistakes, but if we learn from those life lessons, then they are no longer failures or regrets, but instead they become achievements. So don't judge yourself too harshly, you are allowed to make mistakes. After all, you are Human. Delusion is a birthright, as the ego is to free will.

There is no right or wrong. As I said in the beginning, truth is only a matter of perspective. But you must acknowledge the truth when it is presented. To deny your true nature is to become like Carlos, and the man who wants to be buried beside his grandmother. That is a life of regret.

The shame lies within, when we disregard our soul's desire to grow and evolve. Like a bad piece of fruit in the garden, the insects attack it and leave it rotting on the vine. Think of yourself as that piece of fruit, and the insects are your fears.

The fear of being small and alone breeds an egotistical behavior of individuality. You stand alone ate up and rotting away, while the other fruit grows abundantly and commands the attention of the Gardner.

When I find a bad tomato, I pluck it from the vine and toss it in the dirt to grow another day. Like old souls; the seeds from yesterday will return another day.

Reincarnation is the rebirth of a soul in a new body. Like the seeds contained within the infested tomato, we will sprout upon this Earth plain once again, until the time when we mature and ripen, and we find ourselves in a basket upon a festive table, among a mighty celebration.

We will never reach the next level of existence if we continue to depend on someone else to do it for us. Just like the medical profession, doctors and nurses are there to assist us, but in the end it's up to you to heal yourself. The same can be said in regards to a favorite guru, preacher, priest, or a Rabi - they cannot fix it all for us spiritually. That is our responsibility. God resides inside us, not outside of us.

Knowledge is never ending. It is the only thing that separates us humans. The more knowledgeable, the more confident and the less fearful we become.

A book can change your life. When you discover something new, a piece of you dies, as a new life blooms. Once you have new knowledge, you are no longer the same person.

Preparing for death is feeding your spirit something new that lifts it high. Question those old beliefs handed down from your parents. This is your world, not theirs. Don't be afraid to rise above who you once were, or who you are today. You were designed to do just that.

Standing still is suffocating to the spirit. Welcome the new, as in new experiences, and new ideas. Life becomes dull and boring when we dig our heels in, and resist change. Change is meant to be a blessing, not a curse.

Change, and all the little deaths it presents, builds trust. The more we fall to our knees, the more often we are presented with an opportunity to overcome our emotions (fear). Our faith grows with each new challenge, and we then begin to trust in ourselves, because we learn – it's not the end of the world.

This is how we prepare for death. We live it time and time again here on Earth.

THE END

So this is the end my friend. If I am to die tomorrow, know that my passing was a success, for I have planted the seed that was given to me. I have done what I came here to do.

I am not a holy woman or a preacher. I'm just a human being who has been terribly blessed. I stumbled into darkness, and I found the light. I knocked and the door opened; I asked and I received. Yet, I'm far from perfect.

Perfection is a word that should be wiped away permanently from all forms of thought and communication, because there is no such thing, unless we're speaking of a moment in time of course.

The perfect moment is indeed a moment of perfection. It's that ah-ha moment when the light bulb goes off in your head and a new awareness blooms, or that moment when you feel so much love it pours from your eyes, because you can no longer contain it. Moments that make your heart swell, that's what it's all about in the end.

So create an awesome life and make those moments count. For as you grow older you may have less opportunities, but you will always have moments in the past to hold and treasure, and no one can take them away from you.

Writing this book, although intended to assist others on their life journey, has been a healing experience for me. When you heal yourself, you heal the world.

From December 2014 through April 2016, I was pretty much at the mercy of doctors and surgeons. The dream that I began this book with, Fish Food, occurred in the fall of 2016, and it inspired me to share my story.

So I procrastinated in contemplation for a bit and began writing in the winter of 2017. And in a few more weeks it will be fall again. Fall is the time to seed the mind with new endeavors.

So as I bid adieu, I say thank you for being born and choosing to be a part of my world. Much love and many blessings!

REFERENCES:

"The New American Bible," (1987)

"The Biology of Belief," by Bruce Lipton (2008)

"The Healers Manual – A Beginner's Guide to Energy Therapies," Ted Andrews (2003)

"God Within – The Day God's Train Stopped," by Patti Conklin (2014)

"The Practical Encyclopedia of Feng Shui," by Gill Hale (2001)

"The Power of Now," by Eckhart Tolle (1999)

"Animal-Speak," by Ted Andrews (1998)

"Nature-Speak," by Ted Andrews (2004)

"Man's Search For Meaning," by Viktor E Frankl (2006)

"Shamanic Journeying A Beginners Guide," by Sandra Ingerman (2004)

"Victory Over Cancer," by Joseph Marx (2017)

"Natural Healing With Herbs – The First American System of Herbology," by Humbart Santillo, BS, MH (1984)

www.ingramcontent.com/pod-product-compliance
Ingram Content Group UK Ltd.
Pitfield, Milton Keynes, MK11 3LW, UK
UKHW041935190726
13854UKWH00004B/1601

9 781387 248100